WOMEN UNDER STRESS

Randy & Nanci Alcorn

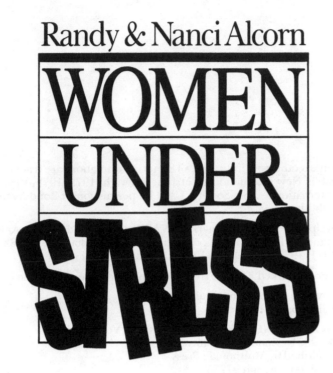

WOMEN UNDER STRESS

Preserving Your Sanity

MULTNOMAH
Portland, Oregon 97266

Unless otherwise indicated, all Scripture quotations are from the Holy Bible: New International Version, copyright 1973, 1978, 1984 by the International Bible Society. Used by permission of Zondervan Bible Publishers.

Scripture references marked NASB are from the New American Standard Bible, © The Lockman Foundation 1960, 1962, 1963, 1968, 1971, 1972, 1973, 1975, 1977. Used by permission.

Verses marked KJV are from the King James Version of the Bible.

Cover design by Judith Quinn
Edited by Liz Heaney

WOMEN UNDER STRESS: Preserving Your Sanity
© 1986 by Randy and Nanci Alcorn
Published by Multnomah Press
Portland, Oregon 97266

Multnomah Press is a ministry of Multnomah School of the Bible.

Printed in the United States of America

Library of Congress Cataloging-in-Publication Data

Alcorn, Randy C.
  Women under stress.

  Includes bibliographies.
  1. Women—Psychology.   2. Stress (Psychology)
3. Women—Religious life.   I. Alcorn, Nanci.
II. Title.
HQ1206.A38   1986   155.6'33   86-18213
ISBN 0-88070-157-9 (pbk.)

89   90   91   —   10   9   8   7   6   5   4   3

To our mothers:

Adele Noren,
always an example of
cheerfulness and servant-heartedness,
and a delight to be with.

and

Lucille Alcorn,
Christ's love and faithfulness personified.
We miss you, Mom,
and look forward to the Great Reunion.

CONTENTS

A PRAYER OF WEARINESS

I am weary, Lord . . . bone-tired.
Weary to the point of tears, and past them.
Your Word says you never grow weary;
But I know you understand weariness
    because once you drug a heavy cross
        up a long lonely hill—
Many times you had nowhere to lay your head—
And people who needed you pressed upon you
    by day and by night.

My reservoir is depleted, almost dry.
For longer than I can remember I've been
    dredging from its sludgy underside
Giving myself and my loved ones the leftovers
    of a life occupied with endless tasks.
The elastic of my life is so stretched out of shape
    that it doesn't snap back anymore.

Just once I'd like to say "It is finished," like you did.
But you said it just before you died.
I guess my job won't be over till my life is
        and that's OK Lord,
    if you'll just give me strength to live it.

Deliver me from this limbo of half-life;
    not just surviving, but thriving.
You who know all, You who know me
    far better than I know myself—
Deposit to my account that as I spend myself
    there may be always more to draw from.

Give me strength
    To rest without guilt . . .
        To run without frenzy . . .
            To soar like an eagle
Over the broad breathless canyons of the life
you still have for me both here and beyond.

ACKNOWLEDGMENTS

We'd like to give special thanks to:

Kathy Duncan, sweet servant and tireless typist;

Kathy Norquist and Theda Hlavka, for their welcome input on the manuscript;

Rainy Takalo, Lyndee Lawrence, John Brose, and Mike Rattray for their helpful professional advice;

Liz Heaney, for all her efforts as our editor;

The women of Good Shepherd Community Church who have allowed us the privilege of ministering to them, and who have so often ministered to us;

Don and Pat Maxwell, whose friendship is always a stress-reliever;

Karina Elizabeth Alcorn and Angela Marie Alcorn, who never cease to challenge and inspire us.

1

SPECIAL STRESSES
ON TODAY'S WOMAN

S tress.
Sometimes it has seemed to be the story of our lives. But it wasn't always that way.

Nanci was raised in a stable, predictable home environment. Her father came home from work the same time every night, dinner was never late, and the phone seldom rang. She ended up marrying a theology student/youth worker/counselor who was about as predictable as a hail storm in July and whose phone sometimes stopped ringing between midnight and sun-up, if she was lucky.

Our early married life brought the usual stresses. Can we afford to go out for pizza? Where do you squeeze the toothpaste tube? Who takes out the garbage? Please put the clothes in the hamper, not in the middle of the floor. We had dated since early high school and developed good communication, so we found the adjustment to marriage wasn't that hard. Having children . . . now that was a different story.

B.C. (Before Children), we were independent. Though we both worked hard and didn't make much money, if we wanted to get up and go have pizza at midnight (can you tell we love pizza?), we did. It was great. Having children was great too—but no more pizza at midnight.

Sleepless nights became the rule instead of the exception. We took turns stumbling into our daughter's room. Just about the time we were getting used to Karina, our first precious attention-demanding gift of God, Nanci was pregnant again. This time her pregnancy was extremely difficult. For the last six months before Angela was born, the slightest wrong move caused excruciating pain in Nanci's pelvis.

Meanwhile, we invited Susan (names have been changed throughout the book), an eighteen-year-old I'd been counseling, to live with us. It was an opportunity to show our love to a non-Christian who needed help and a home. Susan was pregnant, and her boyfriend (the father) was irate about our interference. He later harassed us in various ways. She was a terrific girl—smart, winsome, and fun to be with. It wasn't her fault that her parents hadn't trained her to pick up after herself and to carry her share of the load. After a while Nanci began to feel

14

the pressure (naturally—she was the one home with Susan). Two pregnant women in the same home, one from an unstable background and basically free to come and go with friends all day, and the other overworked and frequently in pain. This was not a storybook arrangement.

Nanci loved Susan—we both did. We had the thrill of seeing her come to Christ while in our home. But the problems were still serious. She stayed out late and failed to live by our household rules.

After a few months, a pattern began to develop. I would come home after a long day of ministry to others only to spend a long night trying to help Susan. Nanci, normally an exceptionally positive and upbeat person, became depressed and emotionally drained. She began to resent Susan and to a degree, me: "You're busy meeting other people's needs—what about mine?"

Worst of all, Nanci felt guilty. She knew she "wasn't supposed to" resent either of us. She knew that what we were doing for Susan was right, and like any good Christian (especially a pastor's wife), she didn't want to violate God's will. She knew all that—but it didn't change the way she felt.

A month after Susan's baby was born—she gave up the baby for adoption to a Christian family—we told her she would have to leave. A little later our baby was born, and the painful pregnancy was over. Nanci's frayed emotions (and mine by that time) began to heal. And then two months after Angie was born, my seemingly healthy mother—and a super grandmother to our daughters—collapsed. In a few weeks she was diagnosed as having terminal cancer.

We brought Mom home from the hospital to live her last days with my father just a mile from our own home. We spent as much time as we could with my rapidly failing mother, to whom we were very close. Nanci and I also needed to give special attention to Karina, our two-and-a-half-year-old, to whom Grandma Alcorn was a second mother.

Mom died two months later. God's grace and comfort penetrated us in powerful ways. But both Nanci and I were still fatigued and emotionally depleted.

15

Soon after, Nanci developed health problems. She was diagnosed as having acute hypoglycemia. She suffered stomach problems, headaches, hives, and what she called a "constant knotted up feeling deep inside." She was losing her hair and at times felt like she was losing her mind.

Meanwhile, I was experiencing insomnia, rashes, chest pains, stomachaches, and other closet illnesses typical of over-committed people (I know that now—I didn't then). By the time I was desperate enough to get a physical examination (men are *so* stubborn—another source of women's stress), I was a walking encyclopedia of stress symptoms.

When my doctor took my blood pressure, he started to write down the figures then did a double take. "This can't be right," he said (doctors should never say that), and took it again. He murmured a "Wow" (doctors should never say that either), and said "You must be extremely tired." He was right. I had exceptionally low blood pressure (rarer than high blood pressure but also a major stress symptom).

When I took a computerized stress test at a medical seminar, I scored in the top 3 percent of my class (no prizes were offered). The note at the bottom said those in my range should consult not only their doctor but "their pastor or counselor." I didn't have the heart to point out my professional title was "Pastor of Counseling."

Nanci and I write from experience. Yes, we've studied stress, taken stress classes, and read innumerable books and articles on the subject. We've counseled with many women under stress. But most importantly, we ourselves have battled with stress. In the process, through failure and success, we've learned a lot about how to pace ourselves so that stress doesn't get the best of us. This book outlines what we have found helpful in coping with stress.

WHY WOMEN?

Stress is the wear and tear of life. It is the cumulative effect of all the demands made on us—physical, mental, emotional and spiritual. Most of the research on stress has been done on men.[1] Nevertheless, stress is just as chronic a problem among

16

women, and in our experience it is most often women who are crying out for help.

While men and women have common stresses, there are significant differences between the sources and kinds of stress they experience. Why? Simply because men and women are so different.

Male-female equality is rooted both historically and theologically in a number of truths. Among these are the common makeup of men and women in the image of God (Genesis 1:27), the biblical mandate to be co-regents over God's earth (Genesis 1:28-30), their mutual identity as Christ's redeemed (Galatians 3:28), their undeniable interdependence (1 Corinthians 11:11-12), and their spiritual partnership in the kingdom of God (1 Peter 3:7). The prominent role of women in Jesus' life and the honor he bestowed them validates their equality to men.

But in the long overdue process of emphasizing gender equality, a terrible mistake has been made. For many, equality has become a synonym for sameness. Every suggested difference between men and women is seen as a threat to female equality. If women are truly equal to men, so goes the logic, they must be virtually the same as men.

No matter how many women invade the traditionally male domain of the work force, no matter how androgynous the current fashions or gender-blended the rock stars, certain things will never change. Women menstruate, men don't. Women become pregnant, men don't. Women produce milk to nurse babies, men don't. Women go through menopause, men don't. These are not cultural differences, they are built-in, created differences; they've never changed and they never will. And each of these differences brings to women a distinctive form of stress that will never be experienced (perhaps not even understood) by men.

These are only the beginning of male-female differences. Men and women are different in countless other ways. Every cell in their bodies is different, because the chromosomes that inhabit those cells are different. Women's metabolisms are different. Their thyroid glands are larger and more active. They

17

have less body hair than men. Normally, their hearts beat faster and their blood pressure is lower.

Women feel pain more than men, but their immunity to disease is higher and they outlive men. Women are built to have a higher percentage of body fat and don't lose weight as easily as men.[2] Men and women are different.

Many of these differences are more than physical. Most men (not all, of course) are less emotional, or at least less emotionally expressive than women. They are also less sensitive. Females are more perceptive of people's true feelings, more easily moved to tears, and quicker to express their feelings. They think more about romance and less about sex than men.

Even from childhood boys and girls are different. Girls usually have greater verbal ability, boys better visual and spatial ability. Girls are normally less aggressive than boys.[3]

Many more men than women suffer heart attacks; more women than men suffer panic and anxiety attacks; far more women than men suffer from agoraphobia (the fear of public places and crowds). Almost three times as many women than men attempt suicide, and twice as many men succeed.

In their landmark book, *Sex and the Brain*, Jo Durden-Smith and Diane deSimone document the significant differences between the male brain and the female brain.[4] Feminist propaganda to the contrary, the fact remains that although men and women are equal, they are very different.

Why all this talk about differentness? Because, given these facts, it should be no surprise to learn that even beyond the reproductive and menstrual processes, men and women's stress experiences are often different.

STRESS AND TODAY'S WOMAN

MY MOTHER THE TAXI

Consider the special stresses on today's mother and homemaker. If air traffic controllers have the most stressful jobs, mothers run a close second. A few near misses a year with planes carrying three hundred passengers is heavy stuff, to be sure. But the mother of young children goes through several near misses a day, with children she values more than hundreds of strangers. How many times do her little ones drop out of trees, tumble down stairs, narrowly miss being hit by cars, step on nails, or burn their tongues on night lights?

Today's mother of school-age children needs the tactical skills of a field marshal. She must get Jimmy ready for school by 8:00 A.M., and be on call in case the car pool driver is ill or can't get her car started. Daughter Jenny goes to a different school that starts at 8:30, but her bus comes at 7:45. Johnny goes to Jenny's school, but he's home at the same time every day (except last week during swimming lessons), whereas she rides the activity bus home two hours later on Tuesdays and Thursdays because of volleyball practice. But on Mondays and Wednesdays there's no activity bus, so she has to be picked up at 5:00—right after Jimmy's trumpet lesson.

Add husband Chuck's erratic work schedule and you have more variables than a physics equation. Despite all this confusion, dinner remains consistent—it is always served somewhere between 4:00 and 7:00 each evening, usually in several shifts, a few in the home and the others at Burger Heaven or Pizza Palace.

Keep in mind we're talking about just one small part of Mom's life. If she can ever get home for more than an hour (wishful thinking), there's ironing piled to the ceiling, dust screaming at her from under the bed, and dried up toothpaste in the bathroom sink. Of course, the rest of the family doesn't notice the housework—unless it doesn't get done.

And if she's ever tempted to conclude that life was easier when the children were younger, it's the proof Mom's been looking for that she's losing her mind.

MOTHERS OF YOUNG CHILDREN

One doctor and stress lecturer has said that the most overstressed person in our society is the mother of small children. Our counseling experience, our family experience, and our conversations with many women confirm this.

Small children are takers. They demand unceasing time, labor, and attention. They cry but can't tell you what's wrong, and when they're old enough to talk they ask you the same question twenty-nine times in a row. They are delightful gifts of God, yes, but "demanding" is their middle name.

Sometimes it seems the children's goal is to see how quickly they can undo all Mom's efforts to clean the house. Kids have an incredible ability to take a box of cereal and spread it evenly over the 200 square feet of living room you vacuumed thirty minutes ago. All this happens while you're cleaning the bathroom. And when you come back to take on the living room again, guess who will lay siege to the bathroom.

No wonder the young mother is so tired—too tired to enjoy a free hour, even if an act of God or congress granted her one. Too tired to think, too tired to exercise, too tired to relax, too tired to eat more than abandoned peanut butter and jelly sandwiches, too tired to make love. Too tired to notice how far she and her husband are drifting apart.

SECONDHAND STRESS

The woman who is mother and wife doesn't simply live with her own stress. She carries the weight of secondhand stress, inherited from her husband and children.

Her husband labors in the work force, struggling with conflicting values and often with his own self-worth, in a society that simultaneously expects too much and too little of him as the household's head. His battles become hers, his hurts hers, his discontent, fears, needs, ego struggles, his burdens—all are hers as well.

Sometimes she feels he's drifting from her. Is he in love with someone else? Two of her friends' husbands have left them. She knows that almost half of all marriages end in divorce. Will hers? Divorce—and the threat of divorce—is a greater pressure on today's woman than ever before.

And what about her children? They're made to grow up too fast. They ask her questions children shouldn't have to ask—questions about serial murders and nuclear war. A child two blocks away was snatched from his own front yard. Mom wants her kids to have fun in the neighborhood, like children should be able to. Yet she finds herself hovering over them, panicking when they disappear even for a moment.

She sees her children sexualized by the media, confused by gender dilution, distressed by accelerated competition at early ages. Mom feels for them and fears for them. She hears sermons that say "Don't worry," yet she still worries about them (now with guilt heaped on worry). She worries about their future, drugs, premarital sex, the school's sex education classes, the violent and immoral rock music her children are inexplicably attracted to. Their needs are hers, their struggles are hers, and when they rebel, it's a knife in her soul.

Mom often acts as the intermediary between her husband and children. She represents each to the other, too often caught in the middle, understanding both but not quite agreeing with either. Confusion. Turmoil. Pressure. Stress.

Single Moms, Widows, and Divorced Women

If the married mother is under all this stress, what about the single mother? She must raise her children *and* engage in the daily battle for bread. She has no one to take turns getting up with a crying child, no one to say, "You've had a rough night—sleep in this morning and let me take the kids."

The physical demands on the single mother are awesome enough, but consider the emotional stresses she lives under. If her husband has died she may struggle with bitterness—"why me? why did *my* husband have to die?" She may want a man's companionship, but feel insecure or even terrified about beginning the whole process of courtship—again. Widowed or divorced, she must learn to handle the family finances, to stretch the dollar as never before, to do household repairs she never used to think about. At a time when she most needs their support, she may feel alienated from her married friends because now she has so little in common with them (she thinks).

In many ways the divorced woman has it harder than the widow. The widow usually doesn't feel guilty for being a failure, or angry at her former husband. The widow has no messy court

21

case to face, no custody battle to leave her exhausted, bitter, embarrassed, or ashamed. And often she has been much better cared for financially.

On the one hand the divorced woman wants her children to have as good a relationship with their father as possible. Yet she may have major reservations about letting them visit their father if he's living with another woman or exposes them to anti-Christian values. And after a weekend with a "Disneyland Daddy" who compensates for his absence by giving them all the fun and food they want, the children come home to their daily routine and the extra chores they've had to take on since their father left. Mom may see herself as competing with Dad—and losing. No wonder she struggles with insecurity, guilt, and resentment.

Of course, the divorced woman without children has her problems too. Most divorced Christian women, and there are many, have the added burden of not knowing where they stand in the Christian community—or knowing that they stand nowhere. The death of a spouse is tragic, but respectable—divorce is not. The church is rightly anti-divorce, but too often comes across as against the divorced individual. Divorced people need special help, support, and guidance from the church. Some flounder, some change churches, some stop going to church at all. When they most need the Christian community, they feel the most alienated from it.

The divorced woman is lonely, and she usually wants to remarry some day. But, biblically, does she have the right to remarry? The right to date? If celibacy is a gift (1 Corinthians 7:7), does God automatically grant it to the divorced person? Should she try one more time to reconcile with her ex-husband, despite his abusiveness to her and the kids? Are other women suspicious of her, thinking she is interested in their husbands? All of these questions spell *stress*.

IT ISN'T EASY BEING LIBERATED

Women are being bombarded in unprecedented ways with all kinds of contradictory messages as to who they are and what they are supposed to look like and act like in today's world.

THE PERVASIVE PRESSURES OF APPEARANCE

Psychology Today compared the results of 1972 surveys and 1985 surveys on how people felt about their bodies and overall appearance. Over 50 percent more women were dissatisfied with their bodies in 1985 than in 1972.[5] In our appearance-centered society, this increasing dissatisfaction is clearly a source of stress.

The mainstays of the American economy are self-improvement products such as makeup, hair spray, hair coloring, perfume, soap, deodorant, and clothing. Since women are the main buyers of self-improvement products, advertisements are geared to women. Their one purpose is, of course, to sell.

Ads must convince the consumer of her need. To do this, they must first persuade her that she is inadequate and incomplete without a particular product. Advertising preys upon, contributes to, and reinforces a woman's poor self-image. As a result, powerful and disturbing feelings of inadequacy tug at a woman's mind—and her checkbook. She buys beauty in the form of soap, attention in the form of perfume, romance in the form of shampoo.

Age spots, split ends, graying hair, and cellulite—fates worse than death, if the media propaganda is to be believed. Years ago, women, while conscious of their appearance, didn't worry about age spots because, though they had them, they didn't know what age spots were. And if they did, they weren't bombarded with warnings about them.

It's not enough for women to wash and brush their hair. Now they are expected to condition it, dye it, color it, curl it, spray it, mousse it, and cut it in fashionable ways. They change hairstyles about as often as their underwear, which itself comes in a multitude of colors and styles. Woman—recreated in the media's image.

Not only is today's woman barraged with this female beauty propaganda, her husband is. Silently, she watches him watch. When she—and he, she supposes—stacks herself up against bronzed bikinied beauties, she sees nothing but a formless slab of whitewashed cellulite. How can she compete? Depression. Stress.

Special Stresses on Today's Woman

The Christian woman is particularly stressed because she knows that enduring values are spiritual, that character is far more important than appearance, and that while people look at the outside, God looks at the inside. But every time she hears a seminar leader (who is usually beautiful) talk about inner beauty, her mind is still on outer beauty. Guilt. Stress.

THE PRESSURES OF WEARING THE SECOND HAT

There is something else today's woman has to face—the constant pressure to leave home to "make something of her life."

Let's face it. Feminists have put homemakers on the defensive. Some women are made to feel guilty for wanting *only* to have a husband and children and oversee a home. They are convinced they need to "get out there in the working world"—as if their world wasn't full of work already.

Mothers often wear the dual hats of homemaker and secretary, wife and executive, mother and salesclerk. Sometimes, simply to prove herself or to support the "wants" that society disguises as "needs," Mom takes the second job. But there's one problem—she is still left with the first.

Enter Super-woman.

Wherever they go—at home or at the office—these women are constantly giving out for the good of others, giving out but not taking in. Reservoirs drained, they live to please others but have nothing left of themselves.

According to research, the major stress vocations are health workers, waiters and waitresses, and nurses.[6] They are constantly serving people—a wonderful calling, but an exceptionally difficult one.

But consider the homemaker. She is health worker and nurse to her children, and often her husband. She is waitress, too.

Whether they work outside the home or not, it's no wonder today's women are under stress. (Women who work both at home and outside as a nurse or waitress—or in a similar serving profession—are particularly vulnerable to stress.)

WHO IS THERE TO SHOULDER YOUR STRESS?

Who is there to take on a woman's struggles, to fight her battles, heal her wounds, listen to her cries? We've found that many women aren't fortunate enough to have sensitive and supportive husbands, or appreciative and helpful children. Even those who do sometimes find themselves feeling misunderstood, alone, afraid, and exhausted.

Then who can shoulder the stress of today's woman? The answer cuts to the very heart of this book, the very heart of coping with stress. It is an answer sadly but inevitably missing from the secular books on stress. Listen carefully:

> Cast all your anxiety on him, because he cares for you (1 Peter 5:7).

Who is this "he" who cares for you? God. The God who cared enough to go to a cross for you . . . who has seen you at your worst and still loves you. The God for whom you need not perform or achieve, but only *be*. The God who knows all, governs all, and weaves all together for your good.

He is the architect, engineer, and builder of all that is you: "Your hands shaped me and made me. . . . Remember that you molded me like clay" (Job 10:8-9). As your designer he knows you as well as a craftsman knows his vase or an author his book. He knows you thoroughly and intimately. "Before I formed you in the womb I knew you" (Jeremiah 1:5).

How does all this relate to stress?

Nanci's father is a structural engineer. He understands how much stress a beam can take, and makes sure that he never gives it a load that exceeds its capacity.

God is our structural engineer. He knows our needs, he knows our load-bearing capacity, our limits. He allows us to live under stress, yes, but never lays upon us a load greater than what he made us to bear.

Special Stresses on Today's Woman

Years ago I ran across a poem by Joe Bayly. I typed it up, placed it on the wall by my desk, and have often contemplated it since. Perhaps it will say to you what it says to me. If it does, it will be worth the price of this book and much more. It's entitled "A Psalm While Packing Books":

This cardboard box
Lord
see it says
Bursting limit
200 lbs. per square inch.
The box maker knew
how much strain
the box would take
what weight
would crush it.
You are wiser
than the box maker
Maker of my spirit
my mind
my body.
Does the box know
when pressure increases close to
the limit?
No
it knows nothing.
But I know
when my breaking point
is near.
And so I pray
Maker of my soul
Determiner of the pressure
within
upon
me
Stop it
lest I be broken
or else
change the pressure rating
of this fragile container
of Your grace
so that I may bear more.[7]

FOOD FOR THOUGHT AND DISCUSSION

1. Do you relate to the authors' experiences with stress? What stress experiences have been most significant in your life over the past several years?

2. Do you agree that there are differences between men and women more basic than what some would have us believe? What are some of life's stresses that men and women share in common? What are some stresses that are unique to women?

3. Does it surprise you to learn that 50 percent more women were dissatisfied with their bodies and overall appearance in 1985 than in 1972? Why or why not?

4. What effects do the media in general and advertising in particular tend to have on a woman's self-esteem?

5. What distinctive stresses fall on each of the following?

teenage girl	single adult woman	young mother
working mother	single mother	divorced woman
widow	middle-aged woman	older woman

6. What stresses on their children do mothers tend to take on themselves?

7. Read 1 Corinthians 10:13 substituting the word *stress* for *temptation*. As your structural engineer, God knows your load-bearing capacity, and he will not let it be exceeded. How does that make you feel?

1. E.g. Meyer Friedman and Ray H. Rosenman, *Type A Behavior and Your Heart* (New York: Fawcett Crest, 1974).

2. Joyce Brothers, *What Every Woman Should Know About Men* (New York: Simon & Schuster, 1981), pp. 36, 39.

3. Eleanor Emmons MacCoby and Carol Magy Jacklin, *The Psychology of Sex Differences* (Stanford, Calif.: Stanford University Press, 1974), pp. 351-52.

4. Jo Durden-Smith and Diane deSimone, *Sex and the Brain* (New York: Warner Books, 1983).

5. Thomas F. Cash, Barbara A. Winstead and Louis H. Janda, "The Great American Shape-Up," *Psychology Today,* April 1986, p. 33.

6. Keith W. Sehnert, *Stress/Unstress* (Minneapolis: Augsburg Publishing House, 1981), pp. 38-39.

7. Joe Bayly, "A Psalm while Packing Books," *Psalms of My Life* (Wheaton, Ill.: Tyndale House, 1969), pp. 13-14. Used by permission.

2

STRESS:
WHAT'S IT
ALL ABOUT?

R uth lives alone and spends most of her days in a dimly lit living room watching soap operas and game shows. She seldom leaves her apartment, has few friends, and is out of touch with her family. Bored with life, she sits and shrivels. Ruth has a problem—too little stress.

We're mistaken if we believe all stress is bad. Without stress there would be no challenges, no accomplishments, no success stories, no art, literature, or athletic feats. Without stress, we would all be unproductive, unmotivated, and uncreative.

Stress provides incentive. Without tests, students wouldn't learn as much. Without guests coming over Friday night, we might not give our house the cleaning it needs, or we might not get out of bed till the crack of noon.

Most of us can't avoid stress, but even if we could we'd be the losers. In fact, there's a name for the complete lack of stress—death. According to Hans Selye, the father of stress research, "Stress is the spice of life."[1]

So what's the problem? The problem—and the reason for this book—is that if stress is the spice of life, many of us are over-seasoned. We have stress to spare—stress running out our ears, running up our blood pressure, and running down our minds and bodies. The problem is not stress *per se*, the problem is we have too much of it.

String a violin too loosely and it won't make good music. String it too tightly and the string breaks. No tension, no music. Too much tension, no music. If our lives are to make music, we must find the balance between too little and too much stress.

WHAT IS STRESS?

Stress is no stranger to you. It was there at your birth when you had your rude introduction to this bright, cold, noisy chaos. Stress was there as a three-month-old when you were wet, hungry, and mad at the world. When you fell down the stairs, got scratched by the kitty, attended your first day of school, played your piano recitals, made your speeches, started your period, went on your first date, got your first job . . . stress was right there. But what exactly is stress?

In our last chapter we briefly defined stress as *the wear and tear of life.* While some researchers give highly specific and technical definitions for stress, to most of us stress is simply a physical and/or psychological sense of pressure or weight, usually triggered by some condition, event, or series of events. Often the word *stress* is used in reference to an external force that places demands on us, such as a stressful occupation, a stressful illness, or a stressful confrontation with a bank teller. But the experts say that stress does not reside in these demands themselves, but in our *response* to these demands.[2]

Suppose you're camping in the woods and see a wolf coming toward your tent. If you're frightened you might think that the wolf is stressful. But it really isn't. To its mate, the wolf means security. And to a mountain man carrying his rifle, one wolf is no threat at all.

Stress is in the eye of the beholder. It's not the wolf that's stressful, it is *we* who are stressful. The wolf simply triggers our stress response, and only then because of our belief—right or wrong—that the wolf poses a threat to us. Likewise, no person or thing or event creates our stress. Stress is rooted in our own response, based on our own perception or interpretation of that person, thing, or event. (We'll take a closer look at this important truth in the following chapter.)

But let's examine what would happen if you really were (heaven forbid) attacked by a wolf. Your mind and body would accelerate and you'd respond instinctively. You might stay and fight with unusual strength. Or you might run with unusual speed (of course, you'd hope the wolf's strength and speed weren't likewise accelerated). Experts call this stress reaction the "fight or flight" response.

When confronted with any threatening situation, your heart beats faster, your blood pressure rises, and adrenaline pumps through your veins. You are energized to deal with crisis—either to face it (fight) or run from it (flight). Either way you are moved to action, and either way you should be thankful for the stress—it may well save your life.

31

We've all heard the stories of mothers picking up cars to rescue their children pinned underneath. This superhuman strength is the result of the mind and body's response to crisis. When the crisis is over, the body returns to normal. It's a good thing, because just as a car engine isn't meant to race continuously, we aren't meant to be constantly mobilized for action. It just isn't natural.

It isn't natural, but unfortunately in our day and age it's common. More and more men and women are characterized by continuously high pulses, high blood pressure, and edgy nerves. It's as if they were constantly traumatized—perpetually hyped up, on call for an emergency. This ongoing condition is called hypertension. And since the body was never meant to maintain such intensity for long, it eventually grinds to a halt. Both conditions—hypertension and exhaustion—are the product of stress.

STRESSORS

Things that trigger stress are called *stressors*. Financial problems, sickness, unemployment, weeks of nasty weather, rebellious children, too many responsibilities, unresolved conflicts, poor communications, lack of solitude, a messy house, family members with busy schedules . . . all of these can be stressors (remember, they can't actually cause stress, but we may respond to them with stress).

Physical and mental problems can trigger stress, and stress can trigger physical and mental problems creating a vicious stress cycle. Some people respond to stress in counterproductive ways—such as overeating, smoking, excessive drinking, and overuse of tranquilizers. But each of these is itself a stressor. In our attempts to relieve stress, we often magnify it.

Stressors come in many varieties—some external and some internal, some in our bodies, some in our minds. Stressors can be as large as losing a loved one, and as small as poorly fitted eye glasses that place unnatural demands on the facial muscles. But large or small, they trigger our stress response, which always takes its toll.

CHANGE AND STRESS

"I just don't know what's wrong with me," Betty sobbed. "I have a good husband, good kids, and I love the Lord. I'm supposed to be happy, but I'm not happy. For the last year it's like I've been slowly sinking in quicksand and it's right up to my chin. I'm getting desperate. And I'm not only miserable, but I feel so guilty for being miserable that it makes me more miserable. What's wrong with me?"

What was "wrong" with Betty stemmed from an accumulation of changes in her life. In the last year her husband changed jobs, they moved to a new neighborhood, they joined a new church, the children changed schools, and her father had major surgery. These changes demanded that Betty adapt, but they came so rapidly that she couldn't adapt. Meanwhile, she had maintained her busy schedule instead of backing off to give herself the time and energy to adjust to the changes. Finally it all caught up with her.

Much of our stress is triggered by change. Change by its nature is disruptive. Physical changes create hormonal and chemical imbalances which can throw us off more than we realize. Both our bodies and our minds thrive on the familiar and seek out their own comfort levels. They fall into certain patterns and like to stay there. We are threatened by whatever is new. That's why change is often so difficult. It requires significant energy for us to adapt to it—physically, mentally, and emotionally.

A major result of this energy drain is increased susceptibility to disease. A research team headed by Dr. Thomas Holmes studied over five thousand patients and concluded that significant life changes greatly increase our likelihood of illnesses. Why? Because *energy needed to fight off infection is used up in the process of adapting to change.*

What kind of change are we talking about? Any kind—but the bigger the change for you, the greater the stress it brings. Here is a list of the changes Dr. Holmes noted in his subjects. The point value attributed to each change—which determines the order in which they're listed—will vary from person to person. Still, the chart is generally accurate and many find it helpful:[3]

33

Stress: What's It All About?

Rank	Event	Life Change Points
1	Death of spouse	100
2	Divorce	73
3	Marital separation	65
4	Jail term	63
5	Death of close family member	63
6	Personal injury or illness	53
7	Marriage	50
8	Fired at work	47
9	Marital reconciliation	45
10	Retirement	45
11	Change in health of family member	44
12	Pregnancy	40
13	Sex difficulties	39
14	Gain of new family member	39
15	Business adjustment	39
16	Change in financial state	38
17	Death of close friend	37
18	Change to different line of work	36
19	Change in number of arguments with spouse	35
20	Mortgage or loan over $10,000	31
21	Foreclosure of mortgage or loan	30
22	Change in responsibilities at work	29
23	Son or daughter leaving home	29
24	Trouble with in-laws	29
25	Outstanding personal achievement	28
26	Wife begins or stops work	26
27	Begin or end school	26
28	Change in living conditions	25
29	Revision of personal habits	24
30	Trouble with boss	23
31	Change in work hours or conditions	20
32	Change in residence	20
33	Change in schools	20
34	Change in recreation	19
35	Change in church activities	19
36	Change in social activities	18
37	Mortgage or loan less than $10,000	17
38	Change in sleeping habits	16
39	Change in number of family get-togethers	15

40	Change in eating habits	15
41	Vacation	13
42	Christmas	12
43	Minor violations of the law	11

Before reading on, put a check next to every event or situation that has happened to you in the last eighteen months. Now, add up your point total. (This is sort of like golf—you're not shooting for a high score, but you need to be honest.)

Did you score less than 150 points? According to Dr. Holmes, you have no more than one chance in three of experiencing a serious decrease in health in the next two years. (Keep in mind that individual tolerance levels vary as much as point levels, so don't swear by this. If your tolerance level is 100 points, you can score 90 and be struggling with stress.)

If you scored between 150 and 300 points, you've scored high. You have an even chance of taking a turn for the worse in your health within the next two years.

If you scored over 300 points you are very vulnerable to disease and even to injury. Why injury? Because injuries are often caused by mental preoccupation and impaired physical responses. In fact, if you did score over 300 points you have an 80 percent chance of facing a major health change in the next two years.

No matter how high you scored, don't despair. It simply means that you must be particularly careful, watch yourself, and make some changes. You should benefit tremendously by applying the stress reduction and coping techniques we will present in this book.

As you went down the scale, you may have been surprised to see that some of the changes were positive. These include marriage, marital reconciliation, pregnancy, gaining a new family member, an outstanding personal achievement, a vacation, and even Christmas. These may be welcome events, but the stress response is very much the same as to unwelcome events—adrenaline increases, blood pressure elevates, and there is a depletion of physical and emotional resources.

Let's apply the stress scale to sixty-three-year-old Gwen. Six months ago her mother passed away in a rest home. John, her husband, retired and soon afterward they moved from Minnesota to Texas. This meant making changes in residence, living conditions, recreation, church activities, and social activities. Suddenly, John died of a heart attack. Within six months, Gwen's change points totaled well over 300.

Whether she realizes it or not, Gwen is at a crisis point. She needs to open herself to God's comfort and encouragement and carefully avoid as many stressors as she can. She also needs the special support, love, and prayers of family and friends—even if she appears to be holding up well.

The Holmes stress scale is a beginning but it is not the last word on the subject of stress. It focuses on *episodic* stress linked to events which don't happen all that often. There is also *chronic* stress, the wear and tear of daily life that may be triggered by things like broken vases, stained carpets, cars that won't start, and checkbooks that won't balance. Psychologist Richard Lazarus maintains that the everyday hassles and annoyances of life actually contribute more to illness and depression than major life changes. So, although a high score probably means you are under stress, a low score doesn't necessarily mean you're not!

STRESS IS CUMULATIVE

One of the most important and least understood characteristics of stress is that it is cumulative. Whether episodic or chronic, whether it involves change or not, all stress has its point values, and those values add up. Often there are significant residual effects of a stressor that came and went as much as a year ago.[4]

Sharon is thirty-six, a strong Christian, and wife and mother of an ideal family. A delightful woman with a quick smile, Sharon is loved by everyone, especially in the church office where she works.

One morning two years ago, Sharon phoned a salesman regarding a photocopy machine the church was interested in buying. Following instructions, Sharon asked the salesman if his company could bring their price down a little. "What do you want us to do," he snapped, "give it to you?"

Sharon wept uncontrollably, unable to finish the conversation. She couldn't move from her desk or drive home, and her husband had to come pick her up. For three months she couldn't come near the church office without the beginnings of an anxiety attack. She couldn't attend church or even go to the grocery store for fear that someone would come up and speak to her. Sharon wondered if she'd ever be normal again.

On the outside, all this seemed strange. How could one rude salesman throw this composed and godly woman into such a tailspin? The truth was that the past year had laid many pressures on Sharon. A dear friend was having serious marriage problems, another friend had turned her back on the Lord, Sharon's father had experienced an emotional breakdown, and she was living amidst a remodeling project that had gone on for a year and a half. Sharon had gone through each of these stressors ministering to everyone who needed her, unaware of the toll it was taking.

Suppose for a moment that Sharon had a stress limit of 200 points. The morning she talked to the salesman she was already at 198. Maybe that conversation was only a three point stressor—but it was enough to take her over her limit.

With strong support from her husband, family, and friends, and a recuperation that included months away from some of her normal responsibilities, Sharon experienced healing. Once she understood the cumulative nature of her stress over the previous year, she wasn't as hard on herself, and gave herself the time and space she desperately needed.

When we understand how stress adds up and why we're a bundle of nerves, why we're exhausted or sick, we are much more prone to take it in stride and allow ourselves to recover. When we don't understand what is happening to us, our stress level increases and we tend to panic, feel hopeless or helpless, and plunge deeper into stress.

Some 200-point women step off the merry-go-round of a hectic life just long enough to let their stress level settle back to a 190, then say, "I feel fine now." But they are still living on the brink. One big stressor, or a few little ones, will send them over again, and this time the results may be more serious. Let your stress level drop significantly before you charge on—and even then be careful, or you're asking for a relapse.

STRESS AND DISEASE

Dr. Holmes's study linked stress to disease. What are some of the diseases stress makes us more vulnerable to?

Harmful, invisible processes take place under stress, including the production of excessive lipids (fat) in the blood. Long-term stress tears down the walls of the arteries. The body responds by laying down cholesterol plaques to repair the damage. If the stress continues long enough, the cholesterol continues to build up and the arteries become more and more narrow and hardened. This restricts the blood flow and therefore demands higher blood pressure in order to get blood to the extremities. This in turn creates more pressure against the arterial walls, resulting in more damage and still more excessive production of cholesterol.

It is this vicious cycle that leads to heart disease, heart attacks, and strokes—the nation's leading killers. (Stress also creates a higher clotting factor in the blood, another leading cause of strokes.)

Government statistics indicate that a full 50 percent of the two million deaths in the United States each year stem from hypertension—often culminated in heart attacks and strokes.[5] That's two deaths every minute, and *that makes stress public health enemy number one.*

Other stress-induced or stress-affected diseases include tuberculosis, multiple sclerosis, leukemia, diabetes, and hypoglycemia. Research has also proven that chronic stress inhibits the body's production of cancer-fighting cells. Many other illnesses we normally think of as purely physical, such as asthma, allergies, and rheumatoid arthritis, are either induced or aggravated by stress. It's as if we carry in our bodies little locked up boxes of potential diseases (which ones may be a matter of genetic proneness) and stress is the key that unlocks them.

Often we fail to see the connection between stress and our most common physical problems. Studies have shown, for instance, that over 90 percent of all headaches are caused by prolonged contraction of the neck muscles, which itself is simply a result of stress.

Many people know the dangers of high cholesterol and attempt to control it by eating less red meat and eggs. That's good. But a single outburst of anger throws us into overdrive and can produce in our bodies the cholesterol equivalent of a dozen eggs!

Stress wears down our immune systems and increases our susceptibility to almost every disease. One year I was under a particularly great amount of stress. I developed a cold and a sore throat during a family vacation in August. The stress did not let up so neither did the illness. I didn't shake it until February—six months later.

Have you ever worked particularly hard for a big occasion—perhaps an important dinner, final exam, or your daughter's wedding—then gotten sick immediately afterward? You've poured out your energy and not enough is left to resist getting sick. You've earned a good illness and now you're going to get it!

Some time ago I discovered I was getting sick almost every Friday—but only on Fridays. Why? Because Friday was my day off. I was working so hard to get everything done by Thursday night that when I finally relaxed my guard on my day off, I was giving my body permission to collapse under the stress I had heaped on it.

STRESS AND MENTAL ILLNESS

While the link between stress and physical diseases is more widely accepted, so-called mental diseases are often just as attributable to stress. We have talked with many women, many Christian women, who say, "I'm afraid I'm losing my mind." Usually these women are perfectly normal and are experiencing perfectly normal stress symptoms. But because they don't know that their anxiety and forgetfulness and inability to concentrate and a host of other problems are stress-induced, their stress is compounded with the fear that they are going crazy. Ironically, it is that fear which often becomes the greatest threat to their mental health. Once they learn proper coping methods, their mental health returns.

Unfortunately, our tendency as Christians is often to treat our material self (body) as totally separate from our immaterial self (called in Scripture the mind, heart, soul, or spirit). In the thinking of many Christians, physical problems are acceptable, but mental and emotional problems are not. We admit we're imperfect physically, but we're ashamed to admit mental and emotional imperfection. Denying these struggles only intensifies them.

Because God has made us whole people, our approach to stress in this book is holistic—recognizing that we are spirit, soul, and body, and that each is critically important and all are interrelated.

ARE YOU UNDER STRESS?

Ever driven on ice? Lost your children in a crowd? You know all too well some of the major stress symptoms!

Stress often shows itself on the face. Nanci and I enjoy watching football (Nanci is the more avid fan), and we often remark about one particular coach. Even when he's winning he's incredibly intense. His brow is constantly furled, his face screwed up and contorted. He looks like a pressure cooker about to explode.

Try standing in front of a mirror. Close your eyes and let your face adopt its normal appearance. Don't smile or contort your face the way you do when you're checking your makeup. Now, open your eyes. Is this a happy, calm, relaxed, and light-hearted face? Or does it reflect tension, impatience, anger, depression?

Now let's take a closer look at your own stress level. Which of these following signs of stress are you experiencing?

Worry
Nervousness
Tension
Irritability
Anger
Impatience
Fears
Insecurity
Insomnia
Irregular breathing
High blood pressure
Low blood pressure
Trembling
Depression
Inability to sit still
Inability to have fun
Lack of contentment
Indigestion
Stomach problems
Headaches
Backaches
Dizziness/lightheadedness
Mood swings
Desire to avoid people
Excessive sleep and naps
Crying spells
Nightmares
Taking tranquilizers
Facial wrinkles
Skin problems (acne, eczema)

Fatigue
Frustration
Hyperactivity
Unexplained itching
Problems swallowing
Heart racing
Heart palpitations
Preoccupation
Restlessness
Loss of concentration
Nervous tics
Ulcers
Unexplained aches and pains
Swings in blood sugar
Inability to relax
Guilt
Helplessness
Hopelessness
Sinking feeling
Irregular bowel movements
Increased allergic symptoms
Increase of appetite
Loss of appetite
Cold hands and feet
Unexplained menstrual changes
Excessive daydreaming
Smoking
Excessive drinking
Unexplained rashes
Frequent colds, sore throats

All of these are red flags, warning signs that something isn't right. We need to view stress and its effects on our bodies and minds like the little red lights on the car's dashboard. When they come on, we've been fairly warned. If we ignore them, it's only a matter of time before we'll be sorry.

So take note of your own little red lights and read on!

THE STRESS-PRONE PERSONALITY

To cope with stress we must not just understand it, we must understand ourselves. The question is not "What is stressful?" but "What makes *me* stressful?" A ride on a roller coaster exhilarates some women, but terrifies others. Some women thrive on weaving their way through noisy, crowded shopping malls, while the very thought of doing so leaves others fearful, tense, irritable, and suffering from migraines. One woman functions best at another woman's breaking point. Socrates said it thousands of years ago and it's still good advice: "Know yourself."

One of the most helpful ways to look at our own vulnerability to stress is in light of the "type A" and "type B" designations popularized by Drs. Friedman and Rosenman in their landmark book *Type A Behavior and Your Heart.*[6] While most of their original research was on men, recent findings indicate that the Type A and B distinctions also apply to women.[7]

Type A's tend to be characterized by most or all of the following:

> Achievement orientation
> Free-floating anxiety
> Time urgency
> Trying to do several things at once
> Excessively high expectations of self and others
> Uneasiness
> Impatience
> Intolerance
> Aggressiveness
> Competitiveness
> Frustration
> Anger
> Strained relationships
> Driven personality
> Guilt feelings when relaxing

Type B's are defined by the absence of these type A traits. The type A is a stress-prone personality with a much higher chance of having heart attacks, strokes, and many other serious ailments. The type B is a stress-resistant personality. Two people may have similar natural temperaments and identical occupations, but one can be a type A and the other a type B. Furthermore, though it's not easy, type A's can become type B's (just as type B's can become type A's) by implementing certain changes in attitudes and behavior.[8]

A type A is preoccupied with the clock. She is afflicted with what Friedman and Rosenman call the "Hurry Sickness." Everything is done quickly, with regular glances at the watch. Type A Martha is impatient and hates to wait in line or in doctors' offices. Type B Mary will make the best of the situation by talking to people in line or writing out a grocery list, and she'll enjoy the wait in the doctor's office by catching up on her reading or knitting.

Type B's are more mellow, low-key, less driven, unhurried, more patient of others, and generally have less to prove than type A's. Not only can they take a vacation, they can have a great time on it. Type B's enjoy life more, and have more time for people. B's tend to be people-oriented, while A's are task-oriented. B's are concerned about life's process, while A's focus on life's products.

It is important to emphasize that type B's can be just as successful as type A's. Ultimately they can be much more successful since they are healthier, happier, and will probably live much longer than type A's. A's run a seven times greater risk of heart attacks than type B's. In fact, type A behavior has been found to precede coronary heart disease 72-85 percent of the time!

Type B's very rarely contract heart disease prior to their seventies, while type A's often develop heart disease in their forties, fifties, and sixties, and sometimes even in their twenties and thirties.

The type A treats life as a 100 meter run—and dies at 150 meters. The type B treats life as a marathon, and paces herself to finish.

The studies show that women who work outside the home are more often type A's than are homemakers, though plenty of homemakers are also A's. Like type A men, these women are more likely than B's to have unhappy marriages.[9]

Not sure whether you're type A, B, or somewhere in between? The following test should help you find out.[10]

Circle the appropriate numbers before each statement. Choose the number on the scale which best describes your usual reaction or behavior. You may use the test to rate yourself or someone else. You can also ask someone to rate you and then compare your answers.

KEY: 1. Never 2. Seldom 3. Sometimes 4. Often 5. Usually

1 2 3 4 5 A. Emphasize or accentuate key words in your ordinary speech, even when it's not necessary to do so.

1 2 3 4 5 B. Speak rapidly to people or utter the last few words of your sentences more rapidly than the opening words.

1 2 3 4 5 C. Move, walk, and eat rapidly.

1 2 3 4 5 D. Feel and sometimes express impatience with the rate at which most events take place.

1 2 3 4 5 E. Attempt to finish other people's sentences before they can.

1 2 3 4 5 F. Become irritated or angry when the car ahead of you is going too slow, you have to wait in line, or you see someone plodding away at a task that you can do faster.

1 2 3 4 5 G. Try to do or think about two or more things simultaneously (such as eating, reading, driving, talking on the phone, etc.)

1 2 3 4 5 H. Find it difficult to refrain from guiding the conversation to those subjects which especially interest and intrigue you. If unable to do this, you pretend to listen but remain preoccupied with your own thoughts.

1 2 3 4 5 I. Feel vaguely uneasy when relaxing for several hours or on vacation for several days.

1 2 3 4 5 J. Fail to observe or appreciate the beautiful or interesting things you encounter in daily life.

1 2 3 4 5   K.   Find that you do not have time to spare on becoming the things worth being because you are so preoccupied with getting the things worth having.

1 2 3 4 5   L.   Attempt to schedule more and more in less and less time, and make fewer allowances for unforeseen contingencies.

1 2 3 4 5   M.   Exhibit nervous tics such as jerking the corners of your mouth, clenching your jaw, or grinding your teeth. (Teeth grinding often happens while sleeping—ask your spouse.)

1 2 3 4 5   N.   Believe that whatever success you have enjoyed has been due to your ability to get things done faster than others.

1 2 3 4 5   0.   Find yourself translating and evaluating your own activities and those of others in terms of numbers. (e.g. How much you make, how fast you run, how many jars of jelly you canned this year, how much you saved on this sale, etc.)

1 2 3 4 5   P.   Competitive in your work or play; winning is important to you.

1 2 3 4 5   Q.   Compare your own or your children's achievements with others.

1 2 3 4 5   R.   Relate aggressively with others, at times even with hostility if you are upset with the person.

1 2 3 4 5   S.   Find yourself rushing out the door, cutting off conversations, and telling your children to "Hurry up."

1 2 3 4 5   T.   Feel uptight and uneasy even when you don't know why.

Add up all the numbers you circled to arrive at your total. If you scored 20-50 you are a type B, if you scored 70-100 you are a type A. If you are between 50 and 70 you are somewhere between an A and a B.

No matter how you scored, you will still experience stress. But remember, type A's needlessly experience much greater stress than type B's, and ultimately they pay the price for it.

If you are a type B, there is still much you can learn about coping with stress. But the closer you are to type A, the more urgent it is that you start learning now. If you are a type A or an in-betweener, by understanding yourself and applying stress reduction techniques you can become a type B, or at least significantly adjust your perspectives and habits. That's what this book is all about.

FOOD FOR THOUGHT AND DISCUSSION

1. How would you define or describe "stress"?

2. What is the "fight or flight" response? What triggers it? How does it affect our bodies and minds?

3. What are some stressors in your life? How and why do you respond stressfully to these particular things?

4. Why does change cause stress?

5. What changes have taken place in your life this last year, and how has each affected you?

6. Using specific illustrations, describe how a person's stress can be cumulative.

7. Why are physical problems more acceptable to people than psychological problems? Does this stigma help or hurt us? How?

8. What stress symptoms do you currently have?

9. What are some of the characteristics of a stress-prone (type A) personality? Are you a type A, a type B, or somewhere in between?

1. Hans Selye, *Stress without Distress* (New York: New American Library, 1974), p. 14.

2. Ibid., p. 83.

3. Thomas H. Holmes and Richard Rahe, "Stress Rating Scale," *Journal of Psychosomatic Research*, 2 (1967): 216.

4. Selye, p. 69.

5. Herbert Benson, *The Relaxation Response* (New York: William Morrow, 1975), p. 18.

6. Meyer Friedman and Ray H. Rosenman, *Type A Behavior and Your Heart* (New York: Fawcett Crest, 1974).

7. Marilyn Elias, "Type A Women Prone to Heart Attacks," *USA Today*, 28 August 1985, p. Al.

8. Jane Brody, "Become a 'Type B'," *Reader's Digest*, April 1981, pp. 87-89.

9. Elias, p. Al.

10. Test adapted from Friedman and Rosenman, pp. 100-102.

3

STRESS, YOUR CIRCUMSTANCES, AND YOUR PERSPECTIVE

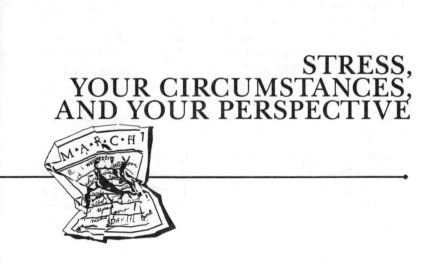

Joyce and Bea both have daughters who married in June. Both women are Christians, both love their girls, both wish them happiness. Although the two weddings were similar, Joyce and Bea had two different experiences.

Joyce was nervous, naturally, but she was excited, joyful, and festive. This wonderful day in her daughter's life was also wonderful for her. Not that everything went smoothly—the wedding coordinator was bossy, the photographer was late, the cake was different than she ordered, and the flowers didn't look quite fresh. When the ring bearer stood on the wrong side of the platform and the groom forgot a line of the vows, Joyce laughed to herself and enjoyed the wedding all the more.

Bea's daughter was married two weeks later in the same church. The wedding went just as well, perhaps a little better. But Bea was uptight, strung out, and ready to string up the photographer, the florist, and the cake decorator for their inexcusable foul-ups. She cringed when the candlelighters didn't stay together, she was fearful that her husband would blow his one line ("Her mother and I"). Her stomach churned when the best man fumbled for the ring. It may have been the happiest day in someone's life, but it was pure misery for Bea. Why? Because of her circumstances? No, because of her *perspective*, her point of view.

Before writing off the difference between Joyce and Bea as "just a difference in personality," think about it. Bea will never be Joyce and shouldn't try to be, but she can learn to develop a positive perspective on life. Indeed, if she is ever to be content and at peace, Bea must change. Unless she does, the same perspective that ruined the wedding for her will inevitably ruin her entire life.

To overcome stress we must either change our circumstances or our perspective on those circumstances. We can change some circumstances, of course, but many we cannot. The truth is that we have little or no control over the photographer, florist, cake decorator, flower girl, or best man. We can't lower taxes, prevent death, make our children get straight

A's, or cause a cease-fire in Central America. We probably can't even get the Book of the Month Club to stop sending us books or our spouse to remove his hair from the bathtub drain.

So if we are to have any peace at all—any relief from stress—we must adjust to human problems, errors, weaknesses, accidents, and any number of things that life is certain to bring and which—if we don't learn to accept them—are certain to drive us nuts.

PERSPECTIVE

Our perceptions—much more than our circumstances—are the building blocks with which we construct our life. There is a sense in which we literally create the world we live in. If it is empty, irritating, boring, hectic, or hurried, it is because we have perceived it that way and thereby made it that way. No matter what the circumstances, our view of life determines our level of joy and contentment.

Don't misunderstand. We are not promoting "positive thinking" for its own sake. Positive thinking is good only when it is biblical thinking.

We know some very ungodly people who are "positive thinkers." They have no time for the doctrine of sin and the reality of true moral guilt and human accountability to God. These things are too "negative" for them. Unfortunately, unless they accept these basic biblical truths, negative as they might be, all the positive thinking in the universe won't deliver them from the ultimate negative—hell.

Neither are we talking about the philosophy behind many of the success books, and the innumerable seminars spun off from them, which define success in terms of the accumulation of wealth (as do many "Christian" sales organizations). They quote freely from Christ and Aristotle and Buddha and "other positive thinkers" and refer to God only in the context of how he can make you wealthy (as if that is his purpose for existing).

All thinking should be rooted in biblical fact. Because of Christ's resurrection, the facts are ultimately positive. The

51

biblicist is ultimately an optimist, not because pop psychology tells him he should be, but because Scripture tells him he should be. The believer's optimism is based squarely on realism: God is real; the incarnation and atonement are real; the second coming is real. We must think positively because the truth is inescapably positive.

Having a biblical perspective is seeing life as God sees it. It is the ability to get past the immediate circumstances to see God's ultimate plan.

Perspective is what Joshua and Caleb had; it's what the other ten spies lacked (Numbers 13-14). Joshua and Caleb entered Canaan and saw the land, the fruit, the potential for prosperity, and a place for their families to live and worship God. The other ten spies went to the same land and saw giants—great men of war, who made conquering the land seem impossible. Of course Joshua and Caleb saw the same giants. But somehow, to them, they just didn't seem so big. The two saw God as bigger than giants. The ten saw giants as bigger than God. Because they saw God on his throne, Joshua and Caleb could look at the same set of circumstances and see a completely different picture than the others saw—a picture both optimistic and realistic.

Our perspective may not be tested in the same way as theirs, but count on it, it *will* be tested.

A few years ago Nanci and I went on a two week vacation to California. We left the kids with friends and took off on what was going to be our greatest vacation ever. We had everything planned and just knew it would all go perfectly.

Everything did go perfectly—for the first forty miles. After that our radiator blew up, costing half a day and half our money to get a new one. Twenty-four hours later the rest of our money and our credit cards were stolen—the Friday evening of Memorial Day weekend. We couldn't wire back for money until the banks opened on Tuesday, three days later, when we had reservations in another part of the state. As the commercials say, "But that's not all." Not only did we have more car problems, but Nanci developed a severe sun rash and couldn't expose her skin to direct sunlight until we returned home to Oregon (where direct sunlight is rarely a problem). Long sleeves, necklines, and floppy hats were the only thing that allowe to escape from the motel.

The point is, while it turned out to be potentially the worst vacation we've ever had, it turned out actually to be one of the best we've ever had. Why? Perspective.

We cried, we prayed, we laughed, we grew. We counted our blessings and realized how much we had and how little we had lost. Once we let go of our ideal picture-perfect vacation and determined to enjoy whatever God had for us, he gave back to us a wonderful time and more. The circumstances didn't improve because our attitudes improved. But, by God's grace, our attitudes completely overwhelmed the circumstances.

As goes our perspective, so goes our vacation, our wedding, our job, our dishes, our ministry, our car pool . . . our whole life.

"Many are the plans in a man's heart, but it is the Lord's purpose that prevails" (Proverbs 19:21). The fulfilled life largely consists of unclenching our fists from our own plans and giving ourselves over to his purpose, whether visible or invisible.

"A man's spirit sustains him in sickness, but a crushed spirit who can bear?" (Proverbs 18:14). A right attitude carries us through bad circumstances and poor health. But no matter how strong the body, how positive the circumstances, a crushed spirit will never experience joy. Perspective is what makes the spirit soar like an eagle even when the body is ravaged by accident, disease, or age.

Stress can't stand in the face of a right perspective.

WHAT WE BELIEVE

Perspective is rooted in belief. We think and act based upon our beliefs. Our belief system is the blueprint around which we build our life and the lens through which we see our life.

This is why exposure to true Bible teaching is so important, and why it's essential both that we attend a church that teaches

God's Word and that we study it daily ourselves. When our beliefs are established on God's truth, the foundation for our entire life is solid and we are more likely to stand despite life's stresses.

When we speak of beliefs, we don't mean merely what we *say* we believe, but what we really *do* believe. Most of us say we believe in a sovereign God. Our doctrine is correct, but the true test of our belief is when we have a week of rain on our long-awaited camping trip, or when the car breaks down on the way to the airport, or the washer—with all of our best delicate clothes in it—is filled with muddy water from a broken water main (this recently happened to Nanci). Is God sovereign when he deals with the rise and fall of empires but not when my tent leaks or my favorite blouse is ruined? Is he sovereign just when I get my way, or is he always sovereign?

Hopefully our beliefs are rooted in truth. But whether they are or not, they will determine our perspective. Ironically, a person going to hell may be relatively happy, while the one going to heaven may be miserable. Both have attitudes based on incorrect beliefs, but whether or not they are correct, beliefs do determine attitudes.

BELIEFS AND FAITH

"But I believe in the sovereignty and love of God, and I'm still unhappy." There is a difference between giving mental assent to Scripture and truly trusting God.

Many of us believe in God to the extent that we would raise our hands if asked, "Do you believe?" But many of us don't really trust him to do what he says he can do. So we stay put because it's safer to maintain the *status quo*—even an unpleasant one—than to step out and trust him.

Trusting God is a matter of faith. "Faith comes from hearing the message, and the message is heard through the word of Christ" (Romans 10:17). We must immerse ourselves in God's Word. Beliefs—right and wrong—form over many years. As a photographic plate accumulates light in a time exposure, faith is firmly established only by regular exposure to the truth and application of that truth to the events we confront in our lives.

Circumstances are but the trigger that call into action our faith. A hard wind doesn't cause a house to be built poorly, but it will likely demonstrate that it was. Likewise the same strong wind that capsizes one sail boat moves another to its destination. Faith thrives in the most adverse circumstance.

REJOICING DESPITE CIRCUMSTANCES

Have you ever read the popular children's story, *Alexander and the Terrible, Horrible, No Good, Very Bad Day?* When you first read the story, you think Alexander did have an unusual number of terrible things happen to him, so no wonder he had a terrible day. But then you realize that the things that happened to Alexander are the usual kinds of irritations that happen to us all daily. They are simply part of being alive in this far-from-perfect world. It is our loss of perspective that magnifies every little thing that goes wrong. Think about it. If today was difficult because "it wasn't a normal day," ask yourself, "When was the last time I had a normal day?" It was not Alexander's circumstances but his interpretation of and response to those circumstances that caused his terrible, horrible, no good, very bad day. Same with ours.

Circumstances aren't what makes a day—or a lifetime—good or bad. Why else are many people with beautiful homes, every material possession imaginable, financial security, and perfect health, miserable . . . even suicidal? And how can many others who live in poverty, own nothing, and have poor health be filled with the joy of life?

Most people rejoice when their circumstances are good, and get depressed when their circumstances are bad. As Christians we are to "rejoice in the Lord always" (Philippians 4:4-6). Do you know what the word translated "always" means in the original Greek? It means always. "Always" means we are to rejoice regardless of our circumstances—not because of them.

As Christians we always have reason to rejoice because of truths that are untouched and unchanged by outward circumstances.

We are created by God, loved by God, cared for by God. "Jesus Christ is the same yesterday and today and forever" (Hebrews 13:8).

Consider Paul and Silas when they were in prison at Philippi. Both men had been severely flogged, and their feet were fastened in stocks in what in those days was surely a disease-ridden, rat-infested cell. How did they respond? "About midnight Paul and Silas were praying and singing hymns to God, and the other prisoners were listening to them" (Acts 16:25). Keep in mind that although Paul and Silas later escaped through divine intervention, at the time they were rejoicing and singing they had no idea they were going to escape. In other words, their spirits were joyful even in the face of further beatings and death.

What would most of us have done in that prison cell? Some of us would mope and grouse and weep and kick the walls and cater our own little pity party. It's when there's something different about us, when we are filled with "the peace of God which transcends all understanding," that we draw the attention of discontented, searching people in need of Christ.

Your baby is born with Down's syndrome or your family business is lost or your spouse leaves or your house is burned to the ground—are we suggesting these circumstances will not affect you? Of course not. We're only saying they need not control you. You can rise above them, as Paul and Silas and many others have done. When these things happen to Christians the world will watch. And if it sees calm in the midst of storm, it will be drawn to Christ.

> Be joyful always; pray continually; give thanks in all circumstances, for this is God's will for you in Christ Jesus (1 Thessalonians 5:16-18).

The choice to give thanks in all circumstances is both cause and effect of a godly perspective.

CRISIS AND TRAGEDY

A *crisis* is an immediate problem with very high stakes that draws our total attention. It may be a terrible accident, the death of a loved one, a son in jail, a church scandal, a daughter who has run away.

Some crises turn out well. The loved one recovers from the accident, the son comes to Christ, the daughter comes home. We may clearly see God's hand in allowing the whole ordeal to happen.

Other times the crisis ends in *apparent* tragedy. Joseph's brothers sold him into slavery and he became a prisoner in Egypt. But years later Joseph could say to his brothers, "You intended to harm me, but God intended it for good to accomplish what is now being done, the saving of many lives" (Genesis 50:20). The moral? If you spell God with a capital *G* you will always spell tragedy with a lowercase *t*.

The prophet Habakkuk understood that there is a joy that transcends all circumstances. Here was a man in a society heavily dependent upon livestock producing, trees bearing fruit, and crops yielding, yet in the midst of his nation's darkest hour he cried out:

> Though the fig tree does not bud
>   and there are no grapes on the vines,
> though the olive crop fails
>   and the fields produce no food,
> though there are no sheep in the pen
>   and no cattle in the stalls,
> yet I will rejoice in the LORD,
>   I will be joyful in God my Savior.
> The Sovereign LORD is my strength,
>   he makes my feet like the feet of a deer,
>   he enables me to go on the heights
>   (Habakkuk 3:17-19).

Few people in all of history have experienced the stress of Jeremiah. His book of Lamentations portrays a vivid and haunting picture of the destruction of Jerusalem and the suffering of her people. After sixty-four of the bleakest verses in God's Word, describing the worst circumstances imaginable, Jeremiah states the obvious. "My soul is downcast within me"

(Lamentations 3:20). But he follows with an amazing response that pulls himself and his reader out of the very depths of hell:

> Yet this I call to mind
>   and therefore I have hope:
> Because of the LORD's great love we
>   are not consumed,
>   for his compassions never fail.
> They are new every morning;
>   great is your faithfulness
> (Lamentations 3:21-23).

Is this kind of perspective in the midst of tragedy restricted to people in Bible times? No! Many women today have exactly the same experience.

Joni Eareckson's swimming accident paralyzed her from the neck down. But if you've read her books, seen her drawings, heard her albums, then you know the beauty of Joni's life. She has not just "made the best" of a bad situation. She has flourished in what God knew was for her the best situation.

A year ago Alice called us: "I'm in a wheelchair now, but God has given me a greater ministry than ever. I pray, I write letters of encouragement, I use the phone to share Christ's love."

You probably know a dozen other women in whose lives God has used tragedy to produce beauty. None of us seek tragedy or welcome it. But it is wise for us to resolve that should apparent tragedy strike—or if it has already—we will let go of our limited perspective and let God prove to us that His promises are true: "Never will I leave you; never will I forsake you" (Hebrews 13:5).

Perhaps you're familiar with the background of the great hymn, "It Is Well with My Soul." The songwriter had just lost his wife and children at sea. The pain was great, but God's grace rose to the occasion. Despite tragedy, the hymnwriter could say without pretense, "it is well with my soul." Only God can perform such a miracle of grace. And only we can stand in the way of his doing so.

THE GIFT OF HOPE

There is a gift God has given his people in all ages that has enabled them not just to hold on, but to experience fulfillment even in times of great difficulty. That gift is hope.

One of the great pervasive themes of Scripture—a persistent melody within a complex musical score—is *waiting on God* (Psalm 27:14; 130:5-6; Proverbs 20:22; Isaiah 8:17; 30:18; Hosea 12:6; Romans 8:23; Titus 2:13). The call to wait on God is a call to faith and hope, believing God that while not all is right, all will be made right. As we daily seek God's face in prayer we must learn to *listen* to him as well as talk to him—to withdraw from the din of man-made clatter and quietly wait as he unfolds to us the certainty of his person, purpose, and plan.

Biblical hope looks beyond the brevity of this life and its troubles. Paul said, "I consider that our present sufferings are not worth comparing with the glory that will be revealed in us" (Romans 8:18). The hope of the people of God is not merely a desire or wish. It is a confidence based on God's promise and God's faithfulness. It is a trust rooted in Christ's trustworthiness and the certainty of his wonderful plan for us:

> Do not let your hearts be troubled. Trust in God; trust also in me. In my Father's house are many rooms; if it were not so, I would have told you. I am going there to prepare a place for you. And if I go and prepare a place for you, I will come back and take you to be with me that you also may be where I am (John 14:1-3).

Jesus does not give us false hope. He guarantees that a day will come when he will reign and all things will be new.

> And I heard a loud voice from the throne saying, "Now the dwelling of God is with men, and he will live with them. They will be his people, and God himself will be with them and be their God. He will wipe every tear from their eyes. There will be no

more death or mourning or crying or pain, for the
old order of things has passed away" (Revelation
21:3-4).

(You've just read the end of the book. So now you know how
the movie's going to turn out.)

The day is coming when all that is wrong will be made right.
All that now hurts shall be healed. All that causes stress, outside
and inside us, shall vanish.

A study was done in which one group of Israeli soldiers was
told they would go on a march, but were not told if or when the
march would eventually stop. Another group was told the
length of the march. They knew there was an end.

Both groups were tested for their stress response. Although they marched not one foot further than those in the
other group, those who did not know whether or when the
march would end registered a much higher level of stress. Why?
Because they had no hope, no tangible assurance that the
forced march would end. They felt helpless—hopeless—won-
dering if they would ever be allowed to rest.

We do not know exactly how long we will be here, but we do
know there will be an end. We will not march forever. We will
rest. That is cause for certain hope. Even in times of greatest
grief Christ leaves us with his hopeful assurance:

> You will grieve, but your grief will turn to joy. . . .
> Now is your time of grief, but I will see you again and
> you will rejoice, and no one will take away your
> joy. . . . I have told you these things, so that in me
> you may have peace. In this world you will have
> trouble. But take heart! I have overcome the world
> (John 16:20, 22, 33).

Hope is the light at the end of life's tunnel. It not only
makes the tunnel endurable, it fills the heart with anticipation
of the world into which we will one day emerge. Not just a better
world, but a new and perfect world. A world alive, fresh, beautiful, devoid of pain and suffering and war, a world without dis-

ease, without accident, without tragedy. A world without dictators and madmen. A world ruled by the only one worthy of ruling.

How do we gain this godly perspective that allows us to see beyond our stress? One way is by seeing how God uses stress itself for his glory and our good. Once we understand that stress is a powerful tool in his loving hand, we will never look at it the same way again.

FOOD FOR THOUGHT AND DISCUSSION

1. Two people can look at the same set of circumstances and have two very different perspectives. Can you think of some challenge or circumstance in your own life to which you could respond either negatively or positively?

2. "To overcome stress you must either change your circumstances or your perspective." Do you agree? Give an example of circumstances that can be changed, and another of circumstances that cannot be changed.

3. What's your opinion of what is often called "positive thinking"? What are its good points? What are its dangers? Should Christians be positive thinkers?

4. Read Numbers 13-14. How does this passage relate perspective to faith in God, and lack of perspective to lack of faith in God?

5. Read Acts 16:16-34. What kind of perspective did Paul and Silas have? How did the other prisoners and the jailer become aware of this perspective? How did it end up influencing the jailer?

6. How would you define "hope" for the Christian? How is it different from what most people call "hope"?

7. How does our knowledge of God's future plan help us face today's stresses with a better perspective?

4

HOW GOD
USES STRESS
FOR YOUR GOOD
AND HIS GLORY

Some years ago Rabbi Harold Kushner wrote the best-seller *When Bad Things Happen to Good People*. He concluded that since there is so much evil and tragedy and suffering, either God must not be all-good or he must not be all-powerful. Opting for God's goodness, he decided God is not all-powerful.

The rabbi's mistake was a familiar one—failure to believe Scripture when it teaches things we do not understand. The truth is that God is all-loving *and* all-powerful and that there are reasons he allows suffering. We cannot understand all those reasons, though sometimes we catch a glimpse of them. But our lack of understanding does not negate God's attributes. It only proves what the Bible said all along.

> "For my thoughts are not your thoughts,
>   neither are your ways my ways,"
>   declares the LORD.
> "As the heavens are higher than the earth,
>   so are my ways higher than your ways
>   and my thoughts than your thoughts"
>   (Isaiah 55:8-9).

We need not and must not hedge on one attribute of God in order to preserve another. He is both holy and loving, both all-good and all-powerful. God cares about the pain and suffering of this world far more than we. One day he will make it all right. Till then we must learn to trust him.

GOD'S PURPOSES AND STRESS

Having a biblical perspective is seeing life through God's eyes. It is seeing order in chaos, use in the useless, and good in the bad. If we are to develop eyes to see God's hand in everything, we must believe (not necessarily understand) what Scripture says about the purpose of stress. *Stress is an effective tool in the hands of our God, a tool that is intended both for his glory and our good.* In this chapter we will look at some ways God uses stress in our lives.

God uses stress to get our attention. God created our bodies. He designed them to send us messages. If I stick my hand in fire, my body will send me a message, quick and clear. If I ignore it, I'll pay the price.

C. S. Lewis said "pain is God's megaphone." Some of us are hard of hearing. We ignore physical, mental, and spiritual warning signs. We're like the stubborn mule the farmer had to hit over the head with a two-by-four, just to get his attention. God wants us to tune our ears to the messages he sends us through our minds and bodies.

God uses stress to help us redefine or rediscover our priorities. Frank and Elaine's marriage relationship was a distant one. They had drifted away from each other over many years, pouring themselves into their jobs and shortchanging their family. But when their son Bill was found in possession of heroin, the months that followed brought unprecedented crisis . . . and also the desire to pull their marriage back together.

Bill isn't doing much better. But Frank and Elaine are doing great! They've rediscovered each other, restructured their lives around the Lord, their family, and their church; they have redefined their priorities in every way. Their marriage has been saved from shipwreck—all as a result of stress and their response to it.

Everyone has priorities. But some of us have never known or experienced the right ones. Our need is to redefine them. Others of us have long known the right priorities. We don't need redefining, but rediscovery. We've tasted right priorities, but we've allowed ourselves to drift away from them. We've replaced fellowship with entertainment, giving with buying, and family time with the television, the lawn, the remodeling job, the causes, and the committees.

By abandoning our God-given priorities we set ourselves up to learn a hard lesson. In essence we do what the Israelites did, living in paneled houses while God's house became a ruin (Haggai 1:4). In response God sent lack of fulfillment, disillusionment, and failure as his messengers. He withheld his blessing till his people rediscovered their priorities:

> Now this is what the LORD Almighty says: "Give careful thought to your ways. You have planted

much, but have harvested little. You eat, but never have enough. You drink, but never have your fill. You put on clothes, but are not warm. You earn wages, only to put them in a purse with holes in it."

This is what the LORD Almighty says: "Give careful thought to your ways. Go up into the mountains and bring down timber and build the house [of God], so that I may take pleasure in it and be honored," says the LORD. "You expected much, but see, it turned out to be little. What you brought home, I blew away. Why?" declares the LORD Almighty. "Because of my house, which remains a ruin, while each of you is busy with his own house. Therefore, because of you the heavens have withheld their dew and the earth its crops. I called for a drought on the fields and the mountains, on the grain, the new wine, the oil and whatever the ground produces, on men and cattle, and on the labor of your hands" (Haggai 1:5-11).

God's people are twice admonished "Give careful thought to your ways." Stress should take us back to the basics. It is an opportunity to reevaluate our priorities and bring them in line with God's.

God uses stress to draw us to himself. Time and again it could be said of the people of Israel, "But in their distress they turned to the LORD, the God of Israel, and sought him, and he was found by them" (2 Chronicles 15:4). It was in Jonah's darkest hour, in his most stressful circumstances that he said this: "In my distress I called to the LORD, and he answered me" (Jonah 2:2). The Psalms are full of references to turning to God, seeking him and finding him in times of intense stress (Psalm 18:6; 81:7; 120:1).

When our lives are comfortable and stress-free, too often we withdraw from the Lord into our own worlds of spiritual independence and isolation. Smug and self-satisfied, we forget what life is really all about. But as the thirsty seek for water, those under stress often seek God. Many non-believers have come to Christ and many believers have returned to him in times of stress.

God uses stress to discipline us. Quoting Solomon's words to his son, the writer of Hebrews offers what he calls a word of encouragement:

> "My son, do not make light of the
> Lord's discipline,
> and do not lose heart when he
> rebukes you,
> because the Lord disciplines those
> he loves,
> and he punishes everyone he
> accepts as a son."

Endure hardship as discipline; God is treating you as sons (Hebrews 12:5-7).

(The word *son*, of course, applies equally to daughters, to all children of God.)

To some of us, this doesn't sound so encouraging. But we fail to realize how essential discipline is. Scripture says that to withhold discipline from a child is to hate a child (Proverbs 13:24). Discipline is corrective. It is remedial, not revengeful. God sends stresses not to get back at us for doing wrong, but to deepen our dependence on him in order to do right. Though the stressful experience may seem excruciating at the time, it is ultimately all for good:

> God disciplines us for our good, that we may share in his holiness. No discipline seems pleasant at the time, but painful. Later on, however, it produces a harvest of righteousness and peace for those who have been trained by it (Hebrews 12:10-11).

God uses stress to strengthen our faith. 1 Peter 1:7 tells us: "These [trials] have come so that your faith—of greater worth than gold, which perishes even though refined by fire—may be proved genuine and may result in praise, glory and honor when Jesus Christ is revealed."

There is only one way a muscle grows—through stress. A muscle that is rarely exercised atrophies; it shrinks into uselessness.

A muscle seldom stretched beyond its usual limits can only maintain itself. It cannot grow. To grow, a muscle must be taxed. Unusual demands must be placed upon it.

Stress is a demand placed upon our faith. Without it our faith will not, *cannot*, grow.

Ever seen grass grow up through asphalt? It's amazing if you think about it. How does grass, pressed flat and robbed of light, persevere through asphalt? Yet we've seen it. Somehow God made those tiny blades of grass to rise to the greatest challenge. We've seen many people rise against odds just as great—people like Sandy, whose husband left her when she was diagnosed with cancer, and who raised her three children all alone.

In the crucible of stress, as we draw on our resources in Christ, we find within ourselves unimagined faith and strength to crack through and rise above the asphalt coat that buries some forever.

LESSONS FROM A STRESSED APOSTLE

The rest of the ways God uses stress we will learn from the apostle Paul, a man who underwent great stress.

> I have worked much harder, been in prison more frequently, been flogged more severely, and been exposed to death again and again. Five times I received from the Jews the forty lashes minus one. Three times I was beaten with rods, once I was stoned, three times I was shipwrecked, I spent a night and a day in the open sea, I have been constantly on the move. I have been in danger from rivers, in danger from bandits, in danger from my own countrymen, in danger from Gentiles; in danger in the city, in danger in the country, in danger at sea; and in danger from false brothers. I have labored and toiled and have often gone without sleep; I have known hunger and thirst and have often gone without food; I have been cold and naked. Besides everything else, I face daily the pressure of my concern for all the churches. Who is weak, and I do not feel

weak? Who is led into sin, and I do not inwardly burn? (2 Corinthians 11:23-29)

God uses stress to teach us contentment.

I know what it is to be in need, and I know what it is to have plenty. I have learned the secret of being content in any and every situation, whether well fed or hungry, whether living in plenty or in want. I can do everything through him who gives me strength (Philippians 4:12-13).

As long as all goes well, as long as we have all we want, we seldom truly appreciate what we have. It is often through loss, often in the fire of stress that we discover God alone is the unfailing source of our contentment. Once learned in times of greatest need, in times of greatest trial, contentment can do for us what is really most difficult—get us through the times of abundance.

God uses stress to develop our perseverance, character, and hope.

We also rejoice in our sufferings, because we know that suffering produces perseverance; perseverance, character; and character, hope (Romans 5:3-4).

James substantiates Paul's claim:

Consider it pure joy, my brothers, whenever you face trials of many kinds, because you know that the testing of your faith develops perseverance. Perseverance must finish its work so that you may be mature and complete, not lacking anything (James 1:2-4).

God's first concern is not about our image, but about our character. Perhaps the greatest measure of character is perseverance—the ability to accept God's dealings in our lives not just for the short run, but for the long haul. Perseverance is not holding on just long enough to get through the crisis. It's learning to live above our circumstances. The same heat that makes some brittle and melts others, tempers still others to make them strong and durable.

God is in the business of turning rough coals into fine diamonds through pressure—stress. When we suffer, it is a God-given opportunity to become more like the One who suffered most.

Hope is both cause and effect of a character that perseveres. Hope is believing in the unseen, trusting in the promise of one who has proven himself faithful. As we read in the previous chapter, hope is living today by tying into God's assurances that tomorrow will be a better day, that God will eventually make all things right—not always in this life, but certainly in the life to come.

Those whose challenges are few in this life see no need to hope for a life to come. They have become comfortable with this world, they have settled into this country. Meanwhile, those whose hope is forged in the crucible of stress are "longing for a better country—a heavenly one. Therefore God is not ashamed to be called their God, for he has prepared a city for them" (Hebrews 11:16).

God uses stress to teach us our inadequacy and his sufficiency.

Paul reveals to us a major source of his stress:

> To keep me from becoming conceited . . . there was given me a thorn in my flesh, a messenger of Satan, to torment me. Three times I pleaded with the Lord to take it away from me. But he said to me, "My grace is sufficient for you, for my power is made perfect in weakness" (2 Corinthians 12:7-9).

Note that Paul's physical affliction—likely an eye disease, but certainly a debilitating ailment—is said to have come from Satan. Yet Paul goes right on to say that God was using it for a good purpose. Even when something comes from Satan, God uses it for our good.

I have diabetes. Without a doubt, the greatest lesson I've learned through it is the lesson of dependence. Every day I must take insulin injections and blood tests. Every time I do, I'm reminded of my own frailty and inadequacy. In an immediate sense I'm dependent on my insulin to live. In an ultimate sense, I'm dependent on God to live. As Jesus said, "Apart from me you can do nothing" (John 15:5).

Learning to be more dependent on him has been worth every moment of discomfort and inconvenience brought on by my diabetes.

In 2 Corinthians 1 Paul says this:

> We do not want you to be uninformed, brothers, about the hardships we suffered in the province of Asia. We were under great pressure, far beyond our ability to endure, so that we despaired even of life. Indeed, in our hearts we felt the sentence of death. But this happened that we might not rely on ourselves but on God, who raises the dead. He has delivered us from such a deadly peril, and he will deliver us. On him we have set our hope that he will continue to deliver us (2 Corinthians 1:8-10).

Paul and his friends were under such great stress that they thought they would die. But God saw them through it. In the process they learned not to lean on themselves but on him. Their own resources gone, they had no choice but to draw on his. He proved himself faithful. The lifelong lesson learned under stress would never have been learned without it.

God uses stress to teach us our need for each other. We often think of Paul as the Lone Ranger, gallivanting solo about the empire, leading everyone to Christ, never afraid, never struggling, often alone, but never lonely.

Scripture corrects this impression as Paul recounts for the Corinthians one of his recent stresses:

> Now when I went to Troas to preach the gospel of Christ and found that the Lord had opened a door for me, I still had no peace of mind, because I did not find my brother Titus there. So I said good-by to them and went on to Macedonia (2 Corinthians 2:12-13).

Did you catch that? This is Paul—the super apostle. He says God opened a door of ministry for him. So what did he do? He went through the door, right? No. He moved on! Paul actually turned his back on a God-given opportunity to minister. Why? Because, he says, "I did not find my brother Titus there."

Paul needed the encouraging presence of a friend. He felt he could go no further without a comrade—someone to listen to him. The principle is clear; when we are isolated from God's family, it's hard to accomplish the tasks of life. And it is often under stress that we turn to our family and friends and find out how much we really need them.

God uses stress to equip us to minister to others. We've seen already that 2 Corinthians is a book about stress. Here's how Paul begins this book (I've put in italics the word *comfort* to emphasize Paul's central thought).

> Praise be to the God and Father of our Lord Jesus Christ, the Father of compassion and the God of all *comfort*, who *comforts* us in all our troubles, so that we can *comfort* those in any trouble with the *comfort* we ourselves have received from God. For just as the sufferings of Christ flow over into our lives, so also through Christ our *comfort* overflows. If we are distressed, it is for your *comfort* and salvation; if we are *comforted*, it is for your *comfort*, which produces in you patient endurance of the same sufferings we suffer. And our hope for you is firm, because we know that just as you share in our sufferings, so also you share in our *comfort* (2 Corinthians 1:3-7).

Paul not only saw God's hand in crisis for his own benefit, but for the benefit of others.

We know women whose heartaches have produced tremendous ministry to others. Linda had a miscarriage and has since ministered to women who've lost children in that way. Denise was the victim of incest and has helped numerous women work through that ordeal. Nanci's hypoglycemia and phobias give her special insights and sensitivities to help others. My mother's death from cancer helped us to understand and more effectively minister to others who've lost their loved ones. My diabetes has likewise opened up doors of ministry.

If you've ever heard Barbara Johnson speak, or read her book *Where Does a Mother Go to Resign?* you've seen how apparent tragedy gives birth to ministry. Barbara's husband was disabled in a terrible accident (she found his body on the road), one of her sons was killed in Viet Nam, a second was killed in a car accident and the third she discovered to be a homosexual. Rather than fold up her faith, Barbara established an outreach to parents, Spatula Ministries, that specializes in encouraging the discouraged.

Stress tugs at the corners of our lives, stretching us always a little more, enabling us to broaden our impact for Christ.

You name the tragedy, the trial, the pressure, the illness, the stress. God can and will use it to expand your ministry to others.

Provided, of course, we let him.

The alternative is nursing a grudge against God, basking in bitterness, or writhing in a slough of self-pity, all of which will leave us shriveled and miserable.

Do All Things *Really* Work Together for Good?

Paul's words in Romans 8:28 best capture the truth so essential to properly responding to life and all its stresses: "And we know that all things work together for good to them that love God, to them who are the called according to his purpose" (KJV).

There was a time when I hated that verse.

Greg was a high school friend. Both of us had known Christ for less than two years. Both of us felt called to the ministry. Then Greg had a terrible accident. All night I sat in the hallway outside the hospital's intensive care unit where he lapsed in and out of consciousness. I prayed with all the faith a young Christian could muster. I claimed every verse and was certain God would heal Greg. A few days later he died.

I was mad at God, and when I heard a minister quote Romans 8:28 to Greg's family (who weren't Christians), I was really mad. For years I associated that verse with senselessness and insensitivity. I resented it, I avoided it, and I hated to hear it.

How things change. Now there is no verse I love more than Romans 8:28.

Paul says, "We know all things work together for good." Not we "guess" or "think" or "wish," but we *know*. Why do we know this? Because we know God. We know that he is all-powerful and all-loving. Since God does the working and he is committed to our good, the only possible conclusion is that all works together for our good. We like the NASB's translation: "God causes all things to work together for good." It's not that things have a way of working themselves out. It's that God has a way of working them out.

The verses that follow Romans 8:28 tell us why all things *must* work together for our good—God has foreknown us and predestined us to become conformed to Christ. Everything that comes our way is part of that process. God makes no mistakes and has no accidents. God never has to say "whoops."

We know *that* all things work together for our good, but "that" doesn't mean we know *how*. When we know who, we don't have to know how. Abraham did not know where he was going when God called him to leave what was familiar (Hebrews 11:8). But he did know with whom he was going.

Does Romans 8:28 really include things that make us suffer? It *especially* includes those things that make us suffer. Back up to Romans 8:18 and get a running start toward verse 28 and you'll see that our present sufferings are precisely what Paul is talking about.

Note what Romans 8:28 does not say. It doesn't say "*each* individual thing *is* good" to those who love God, but "*all* things work *together* for good."

As a boy, I often watched my mother bake cakes. Once, when she had all the ingredients laid out on the counter, I decided to experiment by tasting each one. First the raw flour, then some baking soda, baking powder, vanilla extract, and a spoonful of raw egg. Other than the sugar, everything was repulsive. Even the bittersweet chocolate tasted terrible.

Then I watched as my mother mixed together all those unpalatable ingredients and put them under the intense heat of the oven. The result? A beautiful and delicious cake.

It just didn't make sense to me that the combination of individually distasteful things produced such a tasty product.

It is equally mysterious—but true nonetheless—that God takes all the undesirable stresses in our lives, mixes them together, puts them under the heat of crisis, and produces a perfect result. All things really do work together for good to those who love God. Jesus put it this way: God knows only how to give his children gifts that are good (Matthew 7:10-11).

Perhaps only this can explain the passages of Scripture that say we may not only accept but actually rejoice and delight in suffering (Romans 5:3; 2 Corinthians 12:10). What sounds like spiritual masochism to those who have not experienced it is nothing more nor less than trust in a God who knows no accidents and makes no mistakes in our lives.

In the passage that leads up to Romans 8:28 Paul three times refers to "groaning" under the pains of this life (once, in reference to God's groaning as he identifies with us). He also says, "I consider that our present sufferings are not worth comparing with the glory that will be revealed in us" (Romans 8:18). On the other side of the groan is the glory.

THE WRONG SIDE OF THE TAPESTRY

Ever been to a football game at half time when the band forms words or pictures in the middle of the field? They look great from up in the stands. But have you ever thought about what they look like from the sidelines? Pointless, confusing, apparently meaningless. We see life from the sidelines. God sees it from the stands. As we gain perspective, we leave the sidelines and start working our way up the stands.

It was G. K. Chesterton's character, Father Brown, who said "We are on the wrong side of the tapestry." How true. We see the knots, the snarls, and the frayed underside. But God is on the other side of the tapestry—the side he is weaving into a beautiful work of art. We may not always know what the master artist is doing in our lives. But the important thing is, *he does.*

The greatest way to cope with stress is to accept God's higher purpose in our stress. This is perspective. It means looking beyond the immediate to see the ultimate.

When we see the all-powerful God on the throne of the universe—God our Father committed to our good—we are relieved of much stress. And the stress we must still experience leaves us far richer.

FOOD FOR THOUGHT AND DISCUSSION

1. What are some of the ways you've seen God use stress in your life? In others' lives?

2. C.S. Lewis said, "Pain is God's megaphone." Has God ever used a painful experience to get your attention? When?

3. Has God ever used stress to help you rearrange your priorities or to teach you to be content with what he's given you? When?

4. "God uses stress to teach us our inadequacy and his sufficiency." Do you agree? Can you give an example?

5. "God uses stress to teach us our need for each other." How does God use stress to teach us this?

6. Who do you know or know of who has a thriving ministry to others as a result of some stress they have undergone?

7. What does Romans 8:28 mean to you?

8. "We live on the wrong side of the tapestry." Do you think it's possible in this life to at least get a glimpse of God's side of the tapestry? If so, how?

5

HOW TO
COPE WITH STRESS

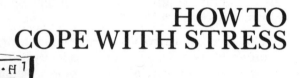

Kristin noticed the lump on her breast but refused to believe it was anything serious. She had a deep fear of cancer and couldn't allow herself to even suspect the lump was a problem. Every week the lump got larger, but every week Kristin managed to ignore it.

One day she went swimming with a friend who noticed the lump and insisted that Kristin see the doctor immediately. The lump was cancerous and by then had spread to the lymph nodes. Had Kristin faced reality months earlier, the cancer probably would have been contained. Through attempting to avoid stress by ignoring and denying the truth, she actually created for herself far more stress.

Many parents ignore serious warning signs in their children because they simply don't wish to believe their little boy is a bully, a troublemaker, or a liar. Ironically, if they would face their child's early symptoms they could take steps to prevent a long-term problem. Instead they protect themselves and their reputation by saying other kids pick on their boy and he's just protecting himself, that his lying is not really lying or that all kids do it or that it's just a phase; meanwhile they do nothing to help him out of this "phase."

How can parents live in the same house with children who are drug addicts and not even suspect it? By being out of touch and by ignoring or denying the symptoms. Denial may save us grief in the short run, but in the long run denial will always magnify grief because the problems continue to fester until they grow to massive proportions.

Denial is just one of many ways we can respond to circumstances that trigger our stress. Another common coping method is escape.

ESCAPE

The escape artist may or may not admit she is unhappy being single or has a poor marriage or an unhealthy self-image or that she is discontent with her life. But she will often avoid reality by stepping into her own fantasy world.

Frequently she is aided in her escape by the media-drugs called romance novels and soap operas, both of which are alarmingly popular among women. A related source of escapism is to follow the fast and loose lives of Hollywood's nymphs and hunks, glamorized through the supermarket tabloids, and *People* magazine and its clones.

A major problem with fantasy is that it actually lures a woman away from the responsibility to accept, deal with, or improve her real world. It promotes materialism through the frequent emphasis on wealth and possessions. It promotes superficiality through the constant emphasis on appearance and outward beauty. It promotes immorality through the relentless elevation of personal pleasure and sexual titillation.

The escapist technique gives the single woman an illusion of intimacy, and helps the married woman find substitutes for her real husband who, when compared to the Prince Charmings of romance land, is a brute or a bore. Silently she transfers her affection to another man, real or imagined. In Robin's case the man was a movie star, in Denise's he was her boss. In order to enjoy sex with their plain vanilla husbands, both women pretended he was someone else, thereby robbing marital sex of its sacredness. Whether single or married, the world of romantic fantasies often includes lust. Jesus labeled this adultery (Matthew 5:27-28). Morality is first a matter of the mind. Anything that would be wrong to do is thereby wrong to fantasize doing.

Certainly a little escapism is good for us all, and our imaginations are a gift from God (what could be wrong with sailing on the Dawn Treader or strolling through Middle Earth?). A mental trip to the beach may be just what the doctor ordered. Relax and enjoy! It should bring us back to reality refreshed and ready to better face the rest of our day. On the other hand, if your dream is going to the Bahamas and that makes you sour or resentful or discontent on your family's camp-out in the state park, then your fantasy has robbed you of appreciating your God-given reality. The acid test of a fantasy (assuming it is not immoral) is whether it brings us back to the real world content and committed to deal positively with our circumstances.

No fantasy is right which feeds our greed. If it leaves us envying others for their wealth, their job, their husband, or anything that is theirs, then it is exactly what God prohibited when he said in the tenth commandment, "You shall not covet your neighbor's house . . . or anything that belongs to your neighbor" (Exodus 20:17). Greed and envy are as stressful as they are wrong.

If we begin to confuse the fantasy world with the real world, we know our escapism has gone too far. A dear Christian friend of ours said, "I knew it was time for me to stop watching soap operas when I found myself praying for the characters."

ACCEPTING, ADAPTING, AND CONTROLLING

The well-known Serenity Prayer says, "God grant me the serenity to accept the things I cannot change, the courage to change the things I can, and the wisdom to know the difference."

If you are attempting to make your parents get along, your boss more understanding, your husband a spiritual leader, or your professor accept Christ, you are taking too much on yourself. You're bound to be frustrated because, while you may be able to influence them (and should certainly try), you *cannot* control them.

If we try to relieve our stress by changing other people, we have fallen for the big lie that the source of our stress—and therefore the solution to it—lies in our environment and in others, not in ourselves.

Perhaps your goal is to get your husband away from his football games to attend church. Or to have him lead a family devotional time. Or to get him to stay on his diet, take you on a vacation, buy a new carpet, or get home every night in time for dinner. These may be fine desires, but they are very poor goals, because goals should be within your power to achieve. By making your goals dependent on others you simultaneously surrender control of your life and attempt to usurp control of theirs.

Mary thought she had to change her husband to be content. Her contentment lay not in her own heart and in the

Christ who dwells there, but in her husband—or in her own persuasive powers. Her attempts to control him—even though with good motives—were manipulative. She was forever prodding him, nagging him, and quarreling with him. The one thing she will probably never succeed in doing is changing him. In fact, she has dominated him and in the process alienated him, multiplying his stress and hers. If he was resistant to change before you can imagine how he digs in his heels now.

The wife who does not understand this principle is spoken of in Proverbs:

> Better to live in a desert
>   than with a quarrelsome and ill-tempered wife
>   (21:19).
>
> Better to live on a corner of the roof
>   than share a house with a quarrelsome wife
>   (25:24).
>
> A quarrelsome wife is like
>   a constant dripping on a rainy day;
> restraining her is like restraining the wind
>   or grasping oil with the hand (27:15-16).

Regardless how spiritual our goal or how sincere our motives, we are playing the role of puppeteer in anyone's life we are demanding to change. And anytime we try to pull the strings of another person, we have crossed over an invisible line.

NOT OURS TO CHANGE

Anne loves her husband and has a wonderful plan for his life. But he has plans of his own and they do not include being remade in Anne's image or in her image of what he should be. Like Anne, many women take upon themselves a messianic role, trying to make changes in their husbands and children and friends that only Christ is capable of making.

Some best-selling women's books, which emphasize the importance of wives submitting to their husbands, actually turn submission into a form of control or manipulation. The subtle or not-so-subtle message adds up to, "Submit to your husband and he'll take you out to dinner, give you flowers, and take you on a nice vacation!" This is giving in order to get. The love and submission Scripture teaches has no ulterior motives, no attempts at controlling or manipulating another human being.

While someone else's change is sometimes in response to our righteous living, we must view it as a by-product. Our purpose must be to please Christ, whether or not anyone responds.

Even if someone we love does change, our problem would not be solved. We might credit ourself with his change and go through life believing that contentment rests in our ability to change people and circumstances. We would then be destined to unhappiness, of course, because we will find out the hard way that many people and circumstances will not change despite our sincerest and strongest attempts to change them.

Sure, we can control certain situations by changing our circumstances. If a job is intolerable, we can leave it for another. If a climate causes allergies, we can move. But most of our problems are not solved by changing our circumstances. I can move from Ohio to California, but if I am unhappy in Ohio I will almost certainly be unhappy in California. Why? Because I am taking myself with me. Happiness and unhappiness do not reside in places but in people. This is why one of the greatest coping skills is learning to adapt to unchangeable circumstances rather than always trying to change, deny, or escape them.

ADAPTING TO THE SEASONS OF LIFE

Surviving stress is largely dependent on the ability to adapt. Sometimes, when it isn't best to fight or flee, the solution is to flow. The more flexible we learn to be, the less distress we will experience.

It is critical that we understand and accept the distinct seasons of our lives. The unmarried college or career woman has certain freedoms the mother of young children does not have. The one wishes she was needed by a family and longs for fewer quiet evenings. The other is tired of being needed by her family and would trade her microwave for the chance to be lonely again.

The young mother longs for the days when her children will be older. The mother of teenagers longs for days past when they were younger or days future when they will be on their own.

The older woman longs for past days of better health. The younger looks forward to the retirement years and the freedom to travel and visit with family and friends.

All these women need to rehearse the advantages and privileges of their present station in life and to accept the fact that they cannot "have it all"—and certainly not all at once.

It is easy to glorify the past and magnify the future. Living in the past and living for the future have one thing in common—they breed discontent with the present. Ironically, only the present is ours. Today is, after all, yesterday's future and tomorrow's past. What we do with today will give us tomorrow's memories, good or bad.

Our tendency is to wish to move on to the next season of our lives, or move back to the last. Sometimes we try to act out our wishes. The mother of young children may find herself acting like a single girl, leaving her house night after night, staying out late with friends, even seeking the attention of other men. But she is in fact "acting"—she is not single and the sooner she comes to accept that fact the better.

Her discontent with her season of life will cause her and her family grief—needless grief. She can learn to thank God for the privileges and the limitations of her present season and circumstances. She can learn to live within the borders of her present country. Once she resolves to do so, she will not only survive but thrive.

WHO'S IN CONTROL?

But stress doesn't just come from trying to change what we can't. It also comes from failing to change what we can. It comes from seeing not just the world around us, but *ourselves* as beyond our control.

This victim mentality is frighteningly prevalent among Christians. Many see themselves afloat on a water-logged piece of a sinking ship, without sail, wind, rudder, life preserver, or the ability to swim to shore or secure the help of others.

While Scripture does not say as much as we would like about circumstance-control, it says a great deal more than we would like about self-control. The Spirit-controlled believer is a self-controlled believer (Galatians 5:22).

Immediately after telling his readers they should cast their anxieties on God, Peter tells them "Be self-controlled and alert" (1 Peter 5:8). Throughout the New Testament we are called upon to exercise self-control. But I cannot exercise self-control unless and until I believe I *can* control myself.

The key to controlling myself is controlling my mind. This is why Solomon said:

> Above all else, guard your heart [inner being, mind],
>   for it is the wellspring of life (Proverbs 4:23).

Paul says to the Romans: "Those who live according to the sinful nature have their minds set on what that nature desires; but those who live in accordance with the Spirit have their minds set on what the Spirit desires" (Romans 8:5).

What is our mindset? That is, what is our mind set upon? Do we dwell on selfish, envious, jealous, bitter thoughts? Or do we dwell on what pleases God? Do we focus on God, his Word, and his mighty works on our behalf, or do we focus on our woes and misfortunes and the abuses we suffer at the hands of others? According to Scripture, the choice is ours.

Time and time again we are told to rid ourselves of wrong thinking and the wrong behavior it leads to, and replace it with right thinking and right behavior (Ephesians 4:22-32; Colossians 3:5-17; 1 Peter 2:1-2; Romans 12:1-2). The underlying idea is that as we are, so should we think, and as we think so should we live.

These passages speak of putting on the new nature in Christ and putting off the old sinful nature. Would God tell us to control our minds and our actions if we are incapable of doing so? Is God so unrealistic or cruel that he would command us to do the impossible?

Peter says, "Prepare your minds for action; be self-controlled. . . ." (1 Peter 1:13). The phrase translated "prepare your mind for action" literally means "gird up the loins of your mind." In the first century, both men and women wore long robes. Confronted with a stressful situation, they would fight or flee. But first they would bend over, grab the back hem of their robe and pull it up between their legs, tucking it in at the belt. They were now prepared to do battle or run without fear of tripping over their robes.

This is what we are to do with our minds—take charge of them, get them in battle condition so we won't trip.

LOSING CONTROL OR SURRENDERING IT?

Jan would not accept Scripture's command to go directly to a woman who had offended her (Matthew 18:15). "I just don't think that's the best way. I can't help how I think, can I?"

Jan had surrendered control of her life to whatever forces "made her think" the way she did. But she was wrong in her belief that we do not have control of the way we think. We can and do control our thoughts. We voluntarily choose to think about certain things, good and bad. We think certain things by decision, other things by default. We think ourselves out of having a milk shake and think ourselves into getting out of bed in the morning.

If we are out-of-control it is only because we have surrendered control. We do not lose control, we relinquish control. We can regain it by accepting our responsibility and taking hold of the reins of our mind.

Jan needed to realize that if Scripture is true, she should accept and obey it. That meant saying no to her old way of thinking and yes to a new way of thinking. Even if she wasn't thinking right, she needed to obey Scripture (that in itself would have eventually changed her thinking). It was not that Jan couldn't change her mind, but simply that she wouldn't.

Consequently, she suffered silently over a situation that could have been resolved if she would have done what she could have done.

CONTROL AND COPING

Stress studies show that a sense of control is essential to mental health. Those who survive captivity with the fewest mental scars are those who maintain as much control as possible even when so much is out of their control. They may treat their cell as a home, rearrange the "furniture," save food and share it with others, write notes to themselves, make plans for their days, order their lives in simple ways. Those prisoners who lose their sense of control lose their purpose, their self-respect, and eventually their minds.[1]

Let's take a closer look, for instance, at the stress that comes our way in the holiday season. Many consider it inevitable and unavoidable.

But in fact much of the stress can be avoided if we: buy Christmas presents far in advance; plan the dinner now, buy the food early and freeze it; structure our calendar and say "no" to extra engagements around Christmas; decide to send fewer Christmas cards, or begin writing them out in September (do wait until December to mail them).

To avoid the Christmas chaos of children opening ten presents in one night, spread out the presents the week before Christmas, letting them open one a day. Or simplify Christmas by making a few simple gifts for each other. Set aside a quiet and peaceful time to read the Christmas story.

This is just a beginning. We can make dozens of other changes. We cannot eliminate all holiday stress of course, but we can certainly minimize it. And if we don't, remember, *it's not because we couldn't but just because we didn't*. It's our own choice. We're no one's victim but our own.

For years I lived under the tyranny of the telephone. I treated the ringing of the phone as divine mandate, and I missed many dinners and bedtime prayers with my daughters because of that phone (no—because of my own choice, *not* because of the phone).

But I've discovered that phone calls are seldom from Mt. Sinai. There are few emergencies and it won't hurt people to call back later.

Now I unplug the phone during dinner and family times. It's my servant, not my master. Frankly, I'm amazed and embarrassed that for many years I let myself be controlled and my family be disrupted by that screaming piece of technology. All needlessly, and all because I didn't take control.

DEALING WITH YOUR OWN STRESSORS

Perhaps Christmas and the telephone aren't a problem for you—but you may lose your job or you're concerned about your friend who is facing a divorce. List several circumstances or situations in your own life that are triggering a stress response. Put them in one of the following categories: uncontrollable, controllable, and partially controllable.

After you have identified the sources of stress and determined whether or not you can control them, you need to make a plan of action. If you can control your stressors, you must determine how. We suggest you go back to your list and look at those things that are controllable or partially controllable. Jot down specifically what you can do about them. Make your plan, schedule the time to do it, then follow through and implement the necessary changes.

While we can't control many things, we can always follow God's formula for dealing with stress by praying about them (Philippians 4:4-6). Sometimes we desperately want to take control when we cannot. But the next best thing to control—no, a better thing—is knowing and trusting the One who is in control.

CAN YOU TAKE CONTROL AND STILL TRUST GOD?

How do self-control and spirit-control relate to each other? How can we reconcile those passages of Scripture that emphasize waiting on a sovereign God with those that emphasize our responsibility to take action? This is a tension that Paul felt, but clearly he saw God at work through his own efforts: "To this end I labor, struggling with all his energy, which so powerfully works in me" (Colossians 1:29).

There is a time to work for change, a time to leave change to God, and a time to accept the fact that change will probably not happen. Our own rule of thumb is "Don't play dead, but don't play God."

Adapt to what you cannot control, control and influence what you can, and leave the rest to him. And remember—when you do, it will be in bigger, better, stronger hands than yours.

FOOD FOR THOUGHT AND DISCUSSION

1. Denial is one attempt to cope with stress. What is the down side of this coping method?

2. Do you think many women escape into a fantasy world to avoid the boredom or unpleasantness of reality? Is this healthy or unhealthy?

3. "Mary thought she had to change her husband to be content." What is the problem with basing your contentment on some other person?

4. Have you ever heard the "submit to your husband" principle taught in a way that is subtly manipulative—implying that if you submit to him you'll get your way or he'll do nicer things for you? What is the danger of this approach?

5. What are some of the distinct seasons of a woman's life? What opportunities and limitations do each of these seasons bring? (Which season are you in right now?)

6. How important is it for a woman to understand and accept her current season in life? What will happen if she doesn't understand and accept it?

7. Though only God is ultimately in control, is it possible to

avoid and relieve some stress by taking better control of our own lives? Give an example.

8. "Adapt to what you cannot control, control and influence what you can, and leave the rest to God." Does this seem like a sound approach to you? Why or why not?

1. Claudia Wallis, "Stress," *Time*, 6 June 1983, pp. 50-52.

6

GETTING
ON TOP OF
YOUR EMOTIONS

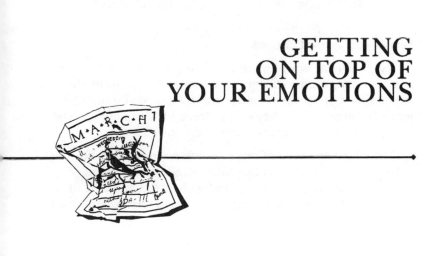

The frightened look in Jenny's eyes told her story even before she described her problem: "My emotions have me on a roller coaster, up one day and down the next. But the ups aren't as high as they used to be, and the downs are getting lower. I'm exhausted, uptight, and scared."

Stress often topples us in the arena of our feelings, and unless we learn to handle them they can bury us. There are many excellent books written about our emotions. It is not our purpose to discuss emotions in depth, but to increase your awareness of your feelings and the impact of their management or mismanagement on your well-being.

First let's consider some basic guidelines for handling our emotions. Then we'll take a closer look at what we believe are the five most stressful emotional states: anger, depression, loneliness, fear, and worry.

What Should I Do with My Emotions?

Recognize Your Feelings

Every person is an emotional being, yet some Christians have been taught that strong emotions are categorically sinful and therefore unacceptable. In and of themselves emotions are neither good nor bad—they simply are. (Questions of right and wrong relate to how we *handle* our emotions.)

Denying that our emotions exist compounds stress. Feeling guilty about our emotions magnifies stress. God created us as rational *and* emotional beings. We feel because he made us to feel. We need to give ourselves permission to feel. (If you need it, let us give you permission!)

Accept Responsibility for Your Feelings

"I can't help how I feel." Not directly, perhaps—we can't make worry and anger disappear just by wishing they would. But we *can* focus on the right thoughts and block out the wrong ones. We can do the right things and refrain from doing the wrong ones. And if we do, our feelings will eventually come into line.

94

If we disclaim responsibility for our feelings and let them dominate our thoughts and actions, we will become out of control. And no one feels stress like one who has surrendered control.

EXPRESS YOUR FEELINGS

Have you ever noticed the safety valve on top of your hot water heater? It's there to release excess pressure. If it wasn't there, the heater could explode.

Expression is our safety valve. The inability to express emotions leaves us bottled up, a hot water heater ready to explode and, in the process, ready to damage not only ourselves but those around us.

Everyone needs a few close friends to talk to openly. When sharing emotions, it is appropriate to share fears, hurts, and even anger, as long as we are careful not to blame or incriminate others.

Studies confirm that crying can be a helpful release of pent-up emotions. There is often truth in the old saying, "I'll feel better after a good cry." Some women—and most men—have an unfortunate stigma about tears. But remember, God created those tear ducts and gave us the ability to cry. Crying is a natural stress reliever. Take advantage of it.

DO WHAT IS RIGHT IN SPITE OF YOUR FEELINGS

God calls us to love others by meeting their needs. Whether we feel warm and fuzzy toward them is beside the point. We don't have to feel a certain way to do what is right.

Perhaps you don't feel respectful toward your husband. Treat him with respect anyway. Maybe you struggle with resentment toward a friend. Send her an encouraging note. Your feelings will eventually follow on the path blazed by your will.

ANGER

Every emotion is powerful and potentially stressful. But nothing so poisons the mind and sours the soul as uncontrolled anger, resentment, and bitterness. Unless we learn to nip these reactions in the bud and learn to forgive others, we will increase our stress level and become embittered.

Anger affects us in different ways. Some of us yell, scream, and bite off heads; others remain outwardly calm while their spleen tremors and their stomach acid sizzles. Some stoop to sarcasm and cynicism. Whether loud or silent, anger is a powerful source of stress. Our blood pressure rises, our cholesterol level rises, almost everything rises except our respect for ourselves and others.

Of course there is such a thing as "righteous anger" (Ephesians 4:26), but the anger we are referring to is the more common unrighteous variety (James 1:20).

Unrighteous anger is counterproductive. It may get the attention of others, but it never wins them over. No husband, no child, no boss, no friend has ever been won over by anger. Anger never unites and resolves. It always alienates and divides. And because of what it does to us physically, it can literally shorten our lives.

Many times anger degenerates into the blame game. Blame is a defense mechanism. I point the finger at you and your faults to get the attention off me and mine. Instead of admitting his own responsibility for his sin, Adam blamed Eve, then Eve blamed the serpent (Genesis 3:11-13). Blame is passing the buck, and it's as old as sin itself.

The blame game has no rules, knows no limits, and spares no victims. Whoever first said "sticks and stones may break my bones but words will never hurt me" was dead wrong. Our bodies heal from sticks and stones, but people's angry words stick in our craw, hurt us, hound us. And so do our own careless words to others. As Solomon said, "Reckless words pierce like a sword, but the tongue of the wise brings healing" (Proverbs 12:18).

The solution? A personal commitment to abandon our self-serving tactics in favor of good wholesome communication.

Communicate. Calmly. Civilly. Often. Communication is a habit that can be changed, a skill that can be developed and improved. It can be worked on and sharpened with amazing results. Pursue the path of positive communication and bypass the detours of anger, bitterness, and blame. You'll be healthier—and so will your loved ones.

Scripture says, "Do not let the sun go down while you are still angry, and do not give the devil a foothold" (Ephesians 4:26-27). The first year we were married Nanci and I agreed never to go to bed angry at each other, even if it meant staying up all night to talk it through. We've stuck with that commitment and it has been the key to short-circuiting many potential resentments that would have eventually led to bitterness (in some ways, the worst of all stresses).

Bitterness often starts with resentment that stems from irritations. Thoughtless words, dirty looks, invitations you didn't receive. These are the beginnings of the malignancy. Perform surgery while they're still small, before the disease spreads.

Scripture says it all:

> Get rid of all bitterness, rage and anger, brawling and slander, along with every form of malice. Be kind and compassionate to one another, forgiving each other, just as in Christ God forgave you (Ephesians 4:31-32).

THE ART OF FORGIVENESS

Forgiveness is the ultimate pain reliever. In forgiving others we unclench our fists and get off the offensive.

Jesus taught that forgiving others is part and parcel of our own forgiveness (Matthew 6:12, 14-15, 18:21-35). Forgiveness is clearly a matter of choice, not feelings. Yes, we may remember the facts of someone's offense, but we must not allow ourselves to dwell on them. We cannot change the past but we can and must change our present attitude toward the past. It is possible to "forgive and forget" if we truly do forgive. But we will never forget what we choose to brood over. And if we allow ourselves to brood, we have not truly forgiven.

Sylvia was repeatedly beaten by her husband. When he abused their daughter, Sylvia finally left him. He has never admitted he was wrong, and never paid a dime of child support. Does he deserve her forgiveness? No. But Sylvia owes it to the Lord, her daughter, *and* herself to work at forgiving him.

Time does *not* heal all wounds. Time alone will only allow the cancer of bitterness to grow. When we refuse to cater to our emotions and refuse to indulge our fatal tendency toward bitterness, only then will time bring healing.

"How will I know if I really haven't forgiven someone?" Do you often think about her offense? Do you throw her sin back in her face from time to time? Do you take opportunities to bring up her offense to others? Do you give her darting glances, dirty looks, or a a cold shoulder? Then you haven't forgiven her. And until you do, you won't be free. It is the unforgiving person—not the unforgiven one—who is truly in bondage. An unforgiving person is invariably a stressful person.

Forgiveness is not unrealistic. The woman whose husband continues in unrepentant adultery is not to pretend nothing is going on. She must exercise tough love and take corrective steps that may even include separating herself and the children from him. Certainly she must let him see that continued sin will take its toll. To whitewash his sin hurts him as much as herself and the children. She should forgive him "seventy times seven," but that does not mean that when he continually rips apart the very fabric of their marriage she will be a party to his sin by keeping up the front of an unbroken home.

It *does* mean that she will pray for his repentance and offer restoration if it comes. It also means that—realizing she cannot control him and he will answer not to her but to God—she will surrender to God her claim on his life. She will refuse to rehearse and dwell on his abuses. Even if he never repents and she never lives with him again, she is called upon to offer him forgiveness.

There is no sin Christ didn't die for, no sin he cannot forgive, and therefore no sin that we, in his strength, cannot forgive.

We must bury the sins of others as God has buried our own (Micah 7:19). And we must commit ourselves never to dig them back up and chew on them, wave them in front of others as gossip, or use them as weapons of revenge or tools to barter and manipulate. If we do, we show we are preoccupied with sin instead of the Savior, and give more credit to its power than to his.

Paul committed himself to forget what was behind and press on to the glorious future God had for him (Philippians 3:13-14). He knew that the only experience comparable to the freedom of being forgiven is the freedom of forgiving.

DEPRESSION

Depression has been called the "common cold of psychological disorders." Twice as many women suffer from depression as men. Nearly three times as many women carry depression to its ultimate extreme by attempting suicide.

Primary warning signs of suicide include withdrawal, personality changes, quiet resignation, and apparent indifference about life. Common circumstances that seem to trigger suicidal thoughts are lengthy illnesses (especially terminal), unemployment, marital and/or family problems. Sometimes the suicidal person talks as if he doesn't expect to be around much longer. If these circumstances or symptoms apply to yourself or someone you know, get professional, spiritual help immediately.

Most depression does not end in suicide, but it is serious nonetheless. Among its physical effects are stomach and bowel pains, changes in appetite, sleep disturbances, aches and pains, and sexual dysfunction. Its mental and emotional effects often include a sense of despair, despondency, and helplessness.

Usually depression is the result of a sense of personal loss. This may be the loss of a loved one, a pet, a possession, money, job, health, a skill, or the loss of one's reputation. Depression almost always involves a negative or deteriorating self-esteem, which amounts to a sense of the loss of one's own personhood. Ultimately, any of these may lead to the worst of all losses—loss of hope.

Negative thoughts preoccupy and dominate the depressed person's mind. Sometimes depression is consciously linked to certain events or circumstances, sometimes not. It often produces withdrawal and fatigue, and can become so debilitating that a person ceases to function normally. That itself leads to further depression.

Depression may stem from physical causes, particularly chemical imbalances. Sometimes it stems from the hormonal imbalances of PMS (Premenstrual Syndrome) or menopause. In such cases both medical and counseling professionals should be consulted. (See chapter 12 for more information on this.)

THOUGHT STOPPING AND THOUGHT SUBSTITUTING

The best way to deal with negative thoughts is to face them head on. Identify the wrong thinking, put your finger on it and say aloud to yourself, "This is wrong—stop thinking it." Some therapists recommend that when wrong thoughts are plaguing you, an effective response is to actually yell loudly, "Stop, stop, stop" (it is preferable not to do this in supermarkets and church services). At least you can whisper to yourself or say the words in your mind. Try it.

Once you say "Stop" to your thoughts, you must substitute them with other thoughts—right thoughts, positive thoughts. This is the principle Paul presents in Philippians 4:8—consciously focus on good thoughts instead of bad ones. Self-talk is telling yourself what is true. It is challenging your false assumptions and replacing them with true ones. It is pulling yourself up by your mental bootstraps. It is being your own therapist. Self-talk can be very effective. In some cases it can also save you $70 an hour!

LONELINESS

Sonia is thirty-five and single. Sometimes painfully single. All of her best friends have gotten married. She used to joke about "always the bridesmaid, never the bride." No more—it hurts too much.

Forty-year-old Elaine carries a secret burden. Her husband Terry is known to others as warm and friendly. Only Elaine and the children see his other side. They walk on egg shells, desperately trying not to trigger his violent temper. Spilled milk, an

100

unironed shirt, a light left on—the slightest offense or accident can launch Terry on a tirade that leaves his family cowering and broken in spirit. On top of everything, he is drinking more and more and plunging the family deeper into debt. Because Terry has refused to get help, Elaine is considering separation. She wants and needs advice, but even more, someone to listen to her, someone to understand her. But, she tells herself, there is no one.

At times all of us are lonely, but to be chronically lonely is to live with almost unbearable stress.

Loneliness may stem from a sense that I cannot be connected with others because I don't deserve it, or because no one would want to link up with someone like me. Poor self-esteem is a major cause of loneliness.

Another cause is individualism. The more we become aware of ourselves as individuals, the more we develop a sense of separation from others. Studies demonstrate that loneliness is more wide-spread and intense in societies which elevate freedom and individuality than in those which elevate corporate solidarity.[1]

The inner person is habitually set aside in our society because secularism, seeing us as different in degree but not in kind from animals, inevitably denies or de-emphasizes our spiritual natures. But it is those natures that have what Pascal called the "God-shaped vacuum, which only he can fill."

When our inner person is unfilled and we are out of touch with our Creator, we are left with a sense of *cosmic* loneliness. We may surround ourselves with people and events and things and activities and noise, but at best these are anesthetics that only cover for the moment the burning pain of our alienation from God—the worst of all lonelinesses.

The ultimate answer to loneliness therefore is theological. We must become connected to the divine reference point who alone gives not only deliverance from sin, but meaning and purpose and personal relationship. Theologically this is called reconciliation. We who were wrong with God are made right with him, we who were distant from him are brought near to him.

What made reconciliation possible? The fact that Jesus Christ became for us the loneliest being in the universe. He became our sin, and for the first and only time in all eternity he was utterly forsaken by his Father (2 Corinthians 5:21, Matthew 27:46). Jesus hung on the cross in all his misery, cloaked in the darkness of absolute aloneness. He experienced the hell of alienation from God so that we would not have to. We can now enjoy the one relationship we most desperately need.

No encounter with a human being can ever replace this ultimate encounter with God.

NEEDING EACH OTHER

On the other hand, we are social beings. We need encounters not only with God, but as one child put it, "Someone with skin on." While the effect of Jesus' incarnation was to put skin on God, the physical Jesus is not now with us to look at and listen to and touch and hug. Yet we are physical beings as well as spiritual, and we need the human touch here and now. This is why each of us in our own way reaches out to others.

No person is an island. We all need to be connected, to belong. We all need a family, one or more people who provide us the support system that helps keep us afloat.

Unfortunately, in many cases the nuclear family has left the extended family a thing of the past. This has isolated many single women who once experienced full membership in a family as sisters and cousins and aunts, but who now feel that the alternative to marriage is loneliness.

Meanwhile the nuclear family is being restructured. One out of four U.S. households with children is now headed by a single parent. In five years the figure may be one out of three, and eventually one out of two.[2] The vast majority of these single parents are women.

One out of every six U.S. women over the age of twenty-one is a widow. Though no one likes to think about it, the fact is that three out of four women will eventually be widowed.[3]

Do most widows adjust to the loneliness that comes with their loss? The American Institute of Stress gives this shocking answer: Widows die at rates 3-13 times higher than non-widows for every known major cause of death. Once again we see that emotional stress dramatically affects physical health.

We need each other more than ever. The Bible emphasizes the priority of caring for widows, orphans, and any others who are unattached to the warmth and security of the family (e.g. Deuteronomy 10:18; 1 Timothy 5:3, James 1:27). We must become more alert to adopting and integrating into our families single women (never-married, divorced, or widowed) who do not have close-knit families or who live far away from their families.

Those of you experiencing the stress of loneliness may need to take the initiative to reach out to a family. Invite them over for dinner. Meet the wife for lunch. Offer to babysit the children. Don't be afraid to say, "I need you," and "I need you to need me."

THE SUPPORT OF SMALL GROUPS

Small groups are therapeutic for many women. They offer an opportunity to minister and be ministered to. If there are eight in the group, one or two may be down today, but the rest can buoy them up.

Small groups often prime the pump and help us to be honest. Nanci and I were in a group with six couples when one woman shared her problems with worry. It was like opening a flood gate. Three other women shared they were struggling with the same thing. It is always encouraging to know you aren't going crazy—or at least someone else is going crazy with you!

Your church may have Bible studies, care circles, growth groups, women's groups, or something similar. If not, start one. Consider forming a reading group that meets weekly or monthly to discuss a book that all the members are reading. This is particularly good for young mothers who are lonely for the intellectual stimulation absent in the world of *The Berenstain Bears Go to the Dentist* and *The Cat in the Hat Comes Back*.

"As iron sharpens iron, so one man sharpens another" (Proverbs 27:17). We need friends not only to avoid loneliness but to grow and mature. David and Jonathan were the best of friends. Here's what happened in David's time of need: "Jonathan went to David at Horesh and helped him find strength in God" (1 Samuel 23:16). What are friends for? For one, to help us turn our eyes to God.

Women who have close friendships wonder how they could get along without them. Other women long for such friendships, yet never seem to find true friends. Why? Perhaps because they are focusing on finding a friend rather than *being* a friend. We will make many friends by being interested in others, but few by trying to get others interested in us.

What's friendship all about? Dinah Mulock Craik (1826-1887) captured it as well as anyone:

> Oh, the comfort—
> The inexpressible comfort—
> Of feeling safe with a person.
> Having neither to weigh thoughts
> Nor measure words,
> But pouring them all right out
> Just as they are,
> Chaff and grain together.
> Certain that a faithful hand
> Will take and sift them;
> Keep what is worth keeping
> And with a breath of kindness
> Blow the rest away.

THE THERAPY OF HELPING OTHERS

One of the best antidotes to loneliness and depression is to reach out to other people.

Sally told us, "We've been in this growth group three months now and not one couple has even invited us over for dinner. I've had it." We asked her a question that apparently had never occurred to her: "How many have *you* invited over for dinner?"

"Well, well . . . none, but . . ." Although Sally had plenty of good excuses, she was unwilling to accept anyone else's.

We have heard many people say, "I stopped coming to

church [or Bible Study] because my needs weren't being met." In our experience, too many people come to get their needs met and too few come to meet needs. If a group of ten people all come to have their needs met, you have a non-needmeeting group. *Somebody* must come not to have their needs met, but to meet the needs of others.

Too many people in the body of Christ are takers. We need more givers. And not to give just in order to get, like Sarah who quit teaching Sunday school because "I was rarely thanked and my name was never even mentioned from the pulpit." True ministers appreciate a pat on the back, of course, but their motive is serving God and others, not getting pats on the back.

This rights-centered society teaches that we find happiness by claiming our rights and focusing on our needs. But in the process of claiming our rights, many of us surrender our responsibilities. God's Word calls upon us to surrender our rights and claim our responsibilities. The essence of both submission and love is sacrifice—surrendering your rights and preferences for the good of another.

Ironically enough, the people who are always out to meet their own needs rarely have them met. Then, when they finally throw themselves into a ministry to others, they wake up one morning and realize, "Hey, my needs are being met."

Ministry is the ultimate form of what psychologist Abraham Maslow calls *self-actualization*. Nothing is more fulfilling than to be used of God to meet the needs of others. When we reach out to others, we get our minds off ourselves and onto them. Helping others has a way of making us feel wanted and needed—it gives us a sense of purpose.

You can begin by visiting someone in the hospital or dropping in at a rest home. Perhaps you could cheer a shut-in, take groceries to the truly poor, or invite a widow over for dinner. If this isn't an established part of your lifestyle, get started—we guarantee you'll be encouraged!

FEAR

Fear comes in many forms. We can fear making the wrong decision or disappointing our friends. We can also fear that our children will be snatched, the car brakes will fail, or the plane will crash.

Our immediate response to a threatening situation—say a loud noise or a scream—is usually a reflexive or involuntary fear. This initial fear is uncontrollable. What we allow to settle into our minds and emotions after our initial response, however, is controllable. If we do not exercise control over it, if we leave the initial fear untamed, it turns into long-term dread or even paranoia.

Whether you suffer from specific phobias, a chronic fear of harm or death to yourself or loved ones, or any other fear, here are some suggestions for coping:

Face your fears by sharing them. Fear thrives most when it lurks in the shadows. Tell someone else and you'll find that fears are more common than you think. Many women suffer from what could be called "fear phobia." They're afraid their fear means they are abnormal.

Amy opened up at a Bible study one night and told the rest of us how "messed up" she was. "It's so bad that when I drive down a road I find myself picturing the oncoming car veering over the line and hitting me head on. I'm really a sicko, aren't I?"

Several in the group laughed out loud. When asked, "How many of you have had the same thing happen to you?" twelve of the fifteen raised their hands. Amy couldn't believe it. The sense of relief was obvious. Just knowing she wasn't abnormal made her fear easier to handle.

Starve your fears—don't feed them. Once a fear is shared, it should not be dwelt on. Talking too much about fears tends to feed or reinforce them, making it more difficult to shake them.

Nanci used to have some recurring thoughts that were morbid and frightening. We would often talk and pray about the problem, but it continued. Finally, concerned that we were reinforcing the thoughts by discussing them, I suggested we stop talking about it. Meanwhile Nanci would continue to recite Scripture and sing hymns whenever the bad thoughts came. From that point on she had victory over those oppressive thoughts and continues to, six years later.

Becky came to Nanci with a problem of obsessive thoughts and dreams about demon possession. Then we found that she had watched some horror movies, including *The Exorcist*. The first item of agenda was to clean up her viewing habits. We can't fill our mind with what is evil and dreadful and then expect not to be bothered by it!

If a woman fears violence to herself and her family, it's better that she doesn't watch violent movies and television programs that feed her fears. For that matter, she'd do better not to read the newspaper or watch the news on television since they major in violent crimes and catastrophes. Studies show that chronic television watchers see the world as being far more dangerous than it really is.

Shift your focus away from your fear and toward God. Read Scripture, memorize it, and pray about your fear. There are hundreds of "fear nots" in the Bible. The most common statement is, "Fear not, for I am with you." God knows our frailties and fears, and he is quick to reassure us:

> Be strong and courageous. Do not be terrified; do not be discouraged, for the LORD your God will be with you wherever you go (Joshua 1:9).

> God has said,
>   "Never will I leave you;
>   never will I forsake you."
> So we say with confidence,
>   "The Lord is my helper; I will not be afraid.
>   What can man do to me?"
>   (Hebrews 13:5-6).

> I sought the LORD, and he answered me;
>   he delivered me from all my fears
>   (Psalm 34:4).

HOW TO CONQUER A PHOBIA

The good news about phobias is that for those who really want to be cured, the cure rate is very high. Seeing a psychologist or psychiatrist is the best approach for many. But there is a proven technique called *systematic desensitization* that some have used to completely overcome their phobias. The following is one way to implement this process.

First take a number of index cards and write down step by step the components of any situation that you find fearful.

Let's say you're agoraphobic, and it is extremely stressful for you to go shopping by yourself. On one 3x5 card write down "Make shopping list." On another write "Put shopping list in purse." Subsequent cards might read "Leave house," "Get in car," "Drive to supermarket," "Get out of car," "Walk to front of store," "Open door," "Enter store," "Walk to meat section," etc. Later cards might include "Line up at the checkstand," "Write out check," . . . "Drive home." The more individual steps you include the better.

Now, lie down and progressively relax your forehead and scalp, facial muscles, neck, shoulders, back, elbows, forearms, fingers, stomach, legs, feet, toes. Let each part of your body become as loose and slack as you can. Imagine the tension draining away. Relax and think of your favorite place—the beach, a mountain cabin, a tree house you had as a child, or whatever. You may wish to play some soft music in the background and turn out the lights. Breathe deeply.

When you are completely relaxed, take the top index card and look at it. Imagine yourself as vividly as you can doing exactly what the first card says—"Put shopping list in purse." If this causes feelings of anxiety, put down the card and focus on relaxing again.

Once you are relaxed again, look back at the same card and visualize the action. If you can remain relaxed while visualizing the action, move to the next card and repeat the process. Remember, don't move forward to the next card if you are no longer relaxed.

Moving slowly, go through as many cards as you can in twenty minutes, but never at the expense of relaxing. Repeat this process daily. You can try picking up where you left off the time before, but you may want to go back a few cards or even to the beginning card and then move through the others more quickly.

Repeat this process until you can imagine the entire scenario, card by card, with little or no anxiety or fear.

By repeatedly rehearsing this formerly fearful sequence of events with a relaxed mind and body, you can completely overcome your phobia! The key to overcoming fear, after all, is in your mind.

Systematic desensitization is not just wishful thinking. It is a proven process that really works. We know from firsthand experience. Until two years ago Nanci had an acute fear of flying which no amount of logic and self-talk seemed to overcome. Because of this fear, Nanci had not been on an airplane since she was in high school, and fully hoped to never get on one again. When two of our dearest friends moved three thousand miles away, then asked us to come and visit, Nanci determined to overcome her phobia.

Through a combination of prayer, Scripture memorization, and systematic desensitization—using the same note card approach we just explained—she made it to the airport, on the plane, and to our friends' house and back. It wasn't easy, but she made it, had a great time, and managed not to lose her sanity—something she could not have imagined before. Nanci says, "If I could overcome such a terrifying phobia, I'm convinced anyone can." (Remember, if you try yourself and don't feel you are progressing, professional counseling can be a great help.)

WORRY

The Greek word for worry means literally "to divide the mind." The worried mind is a torn and therefore worn mind. It is a peaceless mind that doesn't allow itself to rest.

What is there for women to worry about? Erma Bombeck has a few ideas:

I've always worried a lot and frankly, I'm good at it.

I worry about introducing people and going blank when I get to my mother. I worry about a shortage of ball bearings; a snake coming up through the

109

kitchen drain. I worry about the world ending at midnight and getting stuck with three hours on a twenty-four hour cold capsule.

I worry about getting into the Guinness World Book of Records under "Pregnancy: Oldest Recorded Birth." I worry what the dog thinks when he sees me coming out of the shower, that one of my children will marry an Eskimo who will set me adrift on an iceberg when I can no longer feed myself. I worry about salesladies following me into the fitting room, oil slicks, and Carol Channing going bald. I worry about scientists discovering someday that lettuce has been fattening all along.[4]

What can we worry about? Just about anything we choose!

ARE YOU LIVING IN THE PRESENT?

Ironically, much of our worry is unrealistic. We "catastrophize" by making the worst of the situation and anticipating the worst possible outcome. Montaigne, the French philosopher, put it this way: "My life has been full of terrible misfortunes—most of which have never happened."

Much worry comes from carrying today the burdens of yesterday and the dreads of tomorrow. This is unnecessary and unhealthy. Lessons from the past can be learned without living in it. We can plan for the future without dwelling on it. Now is all we have. Let's invest it, enjoy it, profit from it. Let's not lose it to worry.

The most striking characteristic of worry is its absolute impotence. History has no record of worry warding off disaster. No tornado has been prevented, no drought averted, no plane kept from crashing, no child from falling off his bike, no teenager from skipping classes or trying drugs. No heart attacks have ever been avoided through worry (though a great number have been caused by it).

As I write, my brother has been missing for two and a half years. I love him and I'm deeply concerned for him, his health, his safety, his well-being. I must face the possibility of many un-pleasant things, including his death. When my concern degenerates into worry, which it sometimes does, I have to remind myself that my worry will not do him one shred of good, and it will do me considerable harm. This thought relieves me of the sense of obligation to worry, and frees me to move on.

Of course, many things do merit our concern and attention. Our concern for our family's safety can help us take action to enhance their safety. But concern is not worry. Worry is an unhealthy reaction that is ingrown and actually inhibits positive action. Concern is productive—worry is counter-productive.

How to Deal with Worry

Rehearse God's past acts of faithfulness to you. Recount how he provided for you in difficult times. Will he let you down now? Of course not!

> Praise the LORD, O my soul;
> all my inmost being, praise his holy name.
> Praise the LORD, O my soul,
> and forget not all his benefits
> (Psalm 103:1-2).

Count your blessings, not your burdens. You'll find you have much to be thankful for. Worry rarely takes root in a thankful heart.

Bring your worries to God in prayer. "Cast your cares on the LORD and he will sustain you" (Psalm 55:22).

"Cast all your anxiety on him because he cares for you" (1 Peter 5:7).

There are several directions we can cast our worries. We can cast them on ourselves, creating guilt, fear, depression, fatigue, ulcers, and illnesses.

We can cast our worries on others in a negative way, in anger and resentment. This will alienate them from us, and likely contribute to their own worries while not alleviating ours.

We can also share our burdens with others in a positive way. "Carry each other's burdens, and in this way you will fulfill the law of Christ" (Galatians 6:2).

Best of all, we can do what Psalm 55:22 and 1 Peter 5:7 tell us to do—cast our cares on the Lord. His heart is infinitely big and his shoulders are infinitely broad.

Philippians 4:4-7 says it all.

> Rejoice in the Lord always. I will say it again: Rejoice! Let your gentleness be evident to all. The Lord is near. Do not be anxious about anything, but in everything, by prayer and petition, with thanksgiving, present your requests to God. And the peace of God, which transcends all understanding, will guard your hearts and your minds in Christ Jesus.

Long ago there was a stress expert who never charged for his lectures and whose convention centers were the dusty roads and green fields of the countryside. This is what he said about worry. Though many have tried, no one has ever improved on it.

> Therefore I tell you, do not worry about your life, what you will eat or drink; or about your body, what you will wear. Is not life more important than food, and the body more important than clothes? Look at the birds of the air; they do not sow or reap or store away in barns, and yet your heavenly Father feeds them. Are you not much more valuable than they? Who of you by worrying can add a single hour to his life?

> And why do you worry about clothes? See how the lilies of the field grow. They do not labor or spin. Yet I tell you that not even Solomon in all his splendor was dressed like one of these. If that is how God clothes the grass of the field, which is here today and tomorrow is thrown into the fire, will he not much more clothe you, O you of little faith? So do not worry, saying, "What shall we eat?" or "What shall we drink?" or "What shall we wear?" For the pagans run after all

these things, and your heavenly Father knows that you need them. But seek first his kingdom and his righteousness, and all these things will be given to you as well. Therefore do not worry about tomorrow, for tomorrow will worry about itself. Each day has enough trouble of its own (Matthew 6:25-34).

FOOD FOR THOUGHT AND DISCUSSION

1. "I can't help the way I feel." Is this a correct perspective? Why or why not?

2. Is it possible to do what is right even if you don't feel like doing it? Give an example.

3. How does anger affect you personally? How does it make you think, feel, and act? How does it affect you physically? Spiritually?

4. Why do people become bitter? How can you avoid or get rid of bitterness?

5. Have you ever been depressed? What has helped you to deal with feelings of depression?

6. Why do so many people feel lonely? What can we do to overcome loneliness in ourselves and in others?

7. How would you define or describe a true friend?

8. What are some of the fears you have struggled with? What have you done to deal with these fears?

9. Read Philippians 4:4-8 and Matthew 6:25-34, then complete this sentence. "The best reason I can think of for not worrying is _____ ."

1. Craig W. Ellison, "Loneliness," *Baker Encyclopedia of Psychology* (Grand Rapids, Mich.: Baker Book House, 1985), p. 655.

2. "Playing Both Father and Mother," *Newsweek*, 15 July 1985, p. 42.

3. LaVonne Neff, "Three Women out of Four," *Christianity Today*, 8 November 1985, p. 30.

4. Erma Bombeck, *If Life is a Bowl of Cherries—What Am I Doing in the Pits?* (New York: Fawcett Crest, 1971), pp. 10-11.

7

GUILT, GOD, AND SELF-ESTEEM

"**L**ove the Lord your God with all your heart and with all your soul and with all your mind." Jesus called it the greatest commandment, and attached to it a second: "Love your neighbor as yourself" (Matthew 22:37-39).

Jesus linked two loves, one vertical, the other horizontal. One toward God, one toward others.

While Jesus taught two forms of love, he assumed yet another—love for self (love your neighbor *as yourself*). We've seen already our need to reach out to others in love. In this chapter we'll examine both how we should view ourselves and how we can cultivate our relationship with God. Let's begin with a subject very close to home—guilt.

Sin and Guilt

The Hebrew word for sin literally means "to miss the mark." Sin is missing the mark of God's holiness. It is falling short of his righteousness. Some of us fall shorter than others, but all of us fall far short of the goal. "All have sinned and fall short of the glory of God" (Romans 3:23).

Despite what some psychologists would have us believe, there is such a thing as true moral guilt. Therefore, not all guilt feelings are invalid—they may stem from a true condition. We do people no favor by saying "Don't feel guilty" when in fact, according to God's Word, they *are* guilty. Our goal should be a conscience cleansed of sin, not a conscience insensitive to sin.

The unbeliever is alienated from God. She is objectively guilty before him. If she experiences alienation, guilt, and an overall sense of distance from God, she is experiencing what is true. She is actually fortunate to have such feelings—they may draw her to Christ, the only one who can ultimately free her from guilt.

When we, as believers, are living in sin and are therefore out of fellowship with God, we too experience alienation and guilt. Our reconciliation to God through Christ does not change, our future destiny does not change, but meanwhile we cannot enjoy the benefits of our relationship with God. As we

116

sense this condition, it can result in constructive sorrow that leads us to deal properly with our sin (2 Corinthians 7:8-10).

David provides us one of the most vivid descriptions of stress in the entire Word of God:

> When I kept silent [about sin],
>   my bones wasted away
>   through my groaning all day long.
> For day and night
>   your hand was heavy upon me;
> my strength was sapped
>   as in the heat of summer.
> Then I acknowledged my sin to you
>   and did not cover up my iniquity.
> I said, "I will confess
>   my transgressions to the LORD"—
> and you forgave
>   the guilt of my sin (Psalm 32:3-5).

David's health deteriorated; he spent his days sighing and groaning; he felt alienated from God and was left depleted because of unresolved sin in his life. Not all stress comes from sin, but sin is a powerful source of stress.

But there was a solution to David's sin problem, just as there is to ours—"If we confess our sins, he is faithful and just and will forgive us our sins and purify us from all unrighteousness" (1 John 1:9).

David confessed to the Lord the sin that was weighing him down and experienced forgiveness from the guilt that plagued him. The rest of Psalm 32 makes clear that the stress was removed when the sin was dealt with. That is why David was able to write this introduction to the same Psalm:

> Blessed is he
>   whose transgressions are forgiven,
>   whose sins are covered.
> Blessed is the man
>   whose sin the Lord does not count
>   against him
>   and in whose spirit is no deceit (Psalm 32:1-2).

117

Guilt, God, and Self-Esteem

David was forgiven for a host of sins, including adultery and murder. Notice that he had an accurate perception of reality—he felt guilty when he *was* guilty and he felt clean and forgiven when he *was* clean and forgiven.

If we break God's law, as all of us do, we are guilty whether or not we feel guilty. Likewise, once our sins are dealt with in Christ, we are forgiven whether or not we feel forgiven.

RESIDUAL GUILT

Many Christians do not feel forgiven after they have asked for God's forgiveness. They suffer not from true guilt but from residual guilt that saddles their souls.

Helen is one of those Christians. Though she has confessed and genuinely repented of her adultery, she lives in a self-inflicted purgatory. She is convinced God cannot forgive her despite his Word's assurance that he has. God says he has forgotten Helen's sin and has buried it in the deepest sea (Jeremiah 31:34, Micah 7:19). But like the dog who digs up his old bones to chew on them some more, Helen won't let her sin lie where God has buried it. She refuses to accept the atonement. Instead she tries to repeat it.

When Christ died on the cross, he said "It is finished." The word translated "it is finished" was commonly written across certificates of debt—it meant "PAID IN FULL." God insists on paying it all.

God has seen us at our worst and still loves us. None of our sins—past, present or future—are hidden from his sight. No skeleton will fall out of our closets in eternity. God is on our side (Romans 8:31). Jesus is our defense attorney (1 John 2:1). We are therefore teflon saints—no matter who throws dirt at us, it will never stick. In Christ we are totally, absolutely, unconditionally cleared of all our sin.

Jesus suffered for our sins so we would not have to. By refusing to accept his provision, we imply both that he died in vain and that we are good enough to pay our own way to heaven.

FALSE GUILT

Others are plagued by false guilt. False guilt is different from residual guilt, though it has many similar effects. False guilt is a self-condemning, self-punishing response to things for which we are not and never have been truly guilty. False guilt is purely imaginative—but its effects on us are painfully real.

Have you ever driven by a policeman when you weren't doing a thing wrong, yet your heart pounds, your muscles tighten and you breathe rapidly? You treat yourself as if you were guilty even when you aren't! That's false guilt.

False guilt may stem from poor self-esteem, perfectionism, or from unrealistic expectations of one's self. Often these unrealistic expectations are learned early in life, from home or school or church or any number of influences. Sometimes they are simply part of a demanding perfectionistic personality that is instinctively very hard on itself. These personalities can emerge even out of the least demanding environments.

Beneath these unrealistic expectations is often a sense of conditional approval—*if* I succeed in doing all these things *then* God will love me, others will love me, and perhaps I will even love myself. The woman who struggles most from false guilt is often the one concerned about pleasing others and earning their favor, proving to them and to herself she is worthy.

Ironically, false guilt is especially common for the Christian woman. Perhaps it's because she is always reminded of what a godly woman she ought to be, what a submissive, cheerful, organized, and generally stunning wife and mother she's supposed to be. But she knows that she is not all these things—who is? The gap between her expectations and reality is the guilt gap.

Similarly, single mothers may feel guilty because their children don't have a father. Abused women may feel guilty because they feel responsible for their husband's behavior. All of these women expect too much of themselves, and the result is guilt.

Sandra apologizes for everything. If the bread is a little overdone or she has to stay home from church to care for the

119

children or she must excuse herself to answer the phone or change a diaper, Sandra always says "I'm sorry." But she doesn't confine this to little things that don't matter and that everyone understands anyway (so why apologize?). Sandra says "I'm sorry" about the weather, about the lost football game, your headache, about anything and everything that is less than perfect (which covers a lot of ground). And she doesn't just mean "I feel bad for you"—she actually feels responsible for things totally beyond her control. As a result, she labors under a cloud of false guilt.

Denise told me she went to a doctor with terrible stomach ulcers. She put it off far too long, simply because she couldn't bear to admit that she, a Christian, had ulcers (ironically her ulcers were made far worse because she felt so guilty for having them). Her doctor, also a Christian, shocked her with his response: "I find that a higher percentage of my female patients who are Christians have ulcers than those who are non-Christians." Why? Nanci and I believe the answer is unrealistic expectations. We set unattainable goals then punish ourselves for not attaining them.

Some people can feel guilty about anything. Carol said she felt guilty for being happy. She was in a Bible study group where everyone was going through hard times and she wasn't. She felt guilty. So guilty she wouldn't even share the wonderful things God was doing in her life because she didn't want to make everyone else feel bad!

"I SHOULD HAVE"

We have counseled many women who have a bad case of the "I should haves." I should have called, I should have kept Johnny from climbing that tree he fell out of, I should have gone to women's Bible study, I should have attended the wedding, I should have made it to the shower (even though it was the fourth one this month)—I should have, I should have, I should have.

Some stop thinking "I should have" only long enough to think "I shouldn't have." I shouldn't have said no, I shouldn't have gone out with him, I shouldn't have bought that dress, I shouldn't have sent Sarah to school with a runny nose. . . .

Lindy is a missionary who loves to get letters from home, yet goes into a guilt tailspin every time she does because, she says, "I'm so far behind in writing back to so many people."

Valerie felt terribly guilty for backing off from an emotionally needy woman who constantly wanted her attention. But Valerie was busy ministering to other women, as well as her own family. She had to accept the fact that there just wasn't enough of her to go around to everyone who thought they needed her. She was not being selfish—just realistic. Valerie went out of her way to encourage a few others to get together with this needy person. She had been caring and responsible. There was no valid basis for her guilt feelings.

COMBATING GUILT FEELINGS

True guilt can be confessed and dealt with. False guilt is more slippery. No wonder, since Jesus died for our real sins not our imaginary ones.

The only solution to residual guilt is to repeatedly rehearse the facts of forgiveness. Likewise, false guilt is combatted as we rehearse the facts of who we are—and who we are not.

Remind yourself that God cares for you (1 Peter 5:7), God hears you (Psalm 34:15), and God understands your limitations and the stress they bring (Hebrews 4:14-16).

And if you're feeling guilty because you, a Christian woman who "should know better," are going through stress, take a closer look at your Savior. Jesus angrily tossed out the money changers on their ears (John 2:15), was "deeply moved in spirit and troubled" and wept at the death of his friend Lazarus (John 11:33-35), was stirred to compassion by the plight of the multitudes (Matthew 9:36), cried out over his beloved Jerusalem that had rejected him (Matthew 23:37-39). Jesus' stress was so great that the blood vessels under his skin broke and he literally sweated great drops of blood (Luke 22:42-44).

The God-man knew no sin, but he knew a lot of stress. So

the next time you think stress is a synonym for sin, remind yourself of the stress of the sinless one.

UNDERSTANDING AND ACCEPTING WHO I AM

A great deal has been said about self-esteem. Strangely, a preoccupation with self-esteem seems to often undermine self-esteem. Furthermore, the self-esteem movement is showing signs of degenerating into a cult of self-centeredness.

First, we should correct the almost universally accepted notion that Matthew 22:37-39 teaches three kinds of love: God-love, self-love, and others-love. It teaches two kinds of love: that we should love God and that we should love others. It does not teach self-love. It simply recognizes and assumes that self-love exists—and that is something very different than teaching it as a virtue to be cultivated.

In the same way, Ephesians 5 says husbands are to love their wives as their own bodies, but it does not say "husbands, love your own bodies." The one who loves his body takes care of it. He feeds and clothes it. This is self-love—simply to take care of one's self. The biblical authors assumed there was plenty of self-love in almost everyone (we tend to "look out for number one," right?). They were not commanding more self-love but were encouraging their readers to love (take care of) others as much as they already loved (took care of) themselves.

WHO YOU ARE VS. WHO YOU THINK YOU ARE

Rather than emphasize self-love, which can deteriorate into self-centeredness, we need to focus on self-acceptance that is based on an accurate self-image.

It is important to realize the difference between self and self-image. Self is who you really are. Self-image is who you think you are. Who we are determines our destiny, but who we think we are determines the way we live today.

Satan, the master of extremes, wants us either to deify ourselves or degrade ourselves. Scripture tells us it is important to think accurately about ourselves. "Do not think of yourself more highly than you ought, but rather think of yourself with sober judgment. . . ." (Romans 12:3).

Properly understood, Scripture does indeed teach that human beings stand condemned before God. Apart from Christ we are guilty and therefore our self-esteem is naturally low. That is why Christians who try to make people feel fulfilled apart from Christ tread on dangerous ground. Our ministry is not to make guilty people feel less guilty, but to make guilty people know their guilt can be taken away and they can be made righteous by accepting the provision of Christ.

It's only part of the story to say God loves us just the way we are—he also loves us too much to let us stay that way. We are not basically good folks—we are sinners in desperate need of grace. But the bottom line is that God offers that grace. He cleanses us from our guilt and in doing so he gives us the ultimate—and the only—valid basis for a positive self-image. Once God has declared us "not guilty" he says there is no condemnation for us (Romans 8:1). Then and only then should we tell people they should not feel guilty, because in fact they no longer *are* guilty. They are clothed in the righteousness of Christ: acceptable, even commendable in the sight of a holy God.

EXPERIENCING YOUR IDENTITY

Just because God has made us righteous and guiltless doesn't mean we automatically experience the benefits of who we are. Our minds are like tape players, constantly running a message. We see our entire lives in the light of this message. We interpret everything in a way that reinforces our fundamental beliefs about ourselves.

If I think I am Miss Universe, God's gift to everyone, then I interpret everything I do as great, meaningful, more special and significant than what anyone else does. Everything I see reinforces my inflated prideful opinion of myself:

> *I am more important than others. My ideas are always better, my insights more profound, my work more skillful. I am God's gift to the world. Without me, my family and church would crumble. I am indispensable. If I die tomorrow, the*

world would have to close up shop. God needs me on his team, and his work could hardly go on without me. I will always do my best to see that I get all that's coming to me.

This is the kind of attitude that Romans 12:3 warns us not to have when it says, "Don't think more highly of yourself than you ought to think." However, the verse also says we are to think of ourselves with sound judgment, which means we are to think accurately about ourselves. Thinking accurately means that not only are we not to think too highly of ourselves, but neither are we to think too lowly of ourselves. Some women certainly do have a pride problem, but many others have a self-depreciation problem. This is the sort of tape they run through their minds:

I am a failure, a loser from day one. I lack the personality, good looks, brains, or wealth of successful people. I will never be as good as others. I don't do anything right. Nobody likes me, and those that seem to must just be pretending. I am of no use to God. I'm not a worthwhile person and probably never will be.

Both the prideful and the self-depreciating views are a product of a conformed mind, a mind that takes its cues from the world or self rather than from God. The transformed mind is very different. The tape that runs through it says this:

I am not perfect, but I'm immeasurably valuable to God. He specially created me in his image, and I'm unique. Christ thought enough of me to die for me and not consider it a waste.

As a Christian, I'm a child of God. I am clothed with Christ's righteousness. God is on my side. According to his promise, I will spend eternity with him.

God has seen me at my worst and still loves me. This means that regardless of how I feel about myself and how I think others feel about me, I am a priceless human being. I am totally secure in Christ's unconditional and unfailing love. And as long as he still has me here, there's a wealth of purpose and meaning to my life.

Write down these messages, the wrong ones and the right one, and put them in a place where you can regularly look at them (maybe on 3x5 cards taped to your desk, refrigerator, bathroom mirror, or dashboard). As you read through them, consciously reject the wrong messages and consciously accept and meditate on the right one. The more you fill your mind with the biblical truth about who you are, the more your self-image will come into line with your true self.

MADE BY THE MASTER

Facial surgeries, breast implants, and other non-accident-related cosmetic surgeries often betray a sad insecurity that still plagues a woman after they are done. The woman who cannot accept her God-given features does not understand that it is the inner woman God longs for her to cultivate. By focusing on appearance and image rather than character and spirit, many women live in a world of superficiality that ultimately dooms their self-esteem because beauty, as they have wrongly defined it (in outer terms), will inevitably diminish, and with it their acceptance of themselves.

Self-image must be based on what God's Word says is true of us. The world says you are worth a certain amount because you look a certain way or can perform a certain way. God says you are valuable whether or not you can perform by society's numbers. You are not a product of your performance. You may receive a *D* in home ec but *you* are not a *D*. You are an *A*.

Being precedes doing. You are not a child of God if you do everything just right. You are a child of God because, fully aware of all your faults and sins, he has made an irrevocable claim on you to be your Father. God loves you with a love that cannot be earned and therefore cannot be lost. Once you truly understand this, you will experience real security.

The secure woman knows who she is and need not live under the tyranny of self-doubt. Her ego is no longer made out of fine China, but durable stainless steel. Her fear of rejection diminishes, because even when she is rejected she still knows who she is. The fear of failure dissipates, because even when she fails she knows she is still loved. Furthermore, she knows that even her failure is a character-building tool in the hands of the Master Craftsman, who is not yet finished with her.

In Romans 8 Paul spoke to the woman plagued with self-doubt. If we really listen to this message, not once but again and again, it can radically change our lives. Here is the essence of Romans 8:

> Once you come to Christ there is no condemnation for you. You are a child of God who in times of loneliness and hurt can cry to him from the deepest intimacy, "Abba (Papa, Daddy) Father." Both the Holy Spirit and Son pray for you continuously. Your Father filters out everything and only allows you to experience what is for your best good. God is totally on your side; he has chosen you unconditionally and defends you against any accusation. Absolutely nothing you or anyone else can do or say or think will ever, under any circumstances or in any way, separate you from the love of Christ.

CULTIVATING YOUR INNER LIFE

The greatest truth anyone can learn is this: the most important part of your life is the part that only God sees (1 Samuel 16:7; 1 Peter 3:3-4).

In his excellent book *Ordering Your Private World*, Gordon MacDonald compares many Christian lives to Florida sink holes, where buildings and streets appear on the outside to be standing strong, then one day collapse under their own weight because of underground erosion that has left them without support.[1]

Likewise many have made it through life on good looks, talent, and sheer drive, but wake up one day to find that none of those are sufficient to support them under the weight of the stress that has invaded their lives. Keri was one such woman—a successful businesswoman, homemaker, and Bible study leader, she collapsed under the weight of her own success. She admitted to us that for many months the inner garden of her soul had been neglected. Now it had all caught up with her.

Time must be budgeted daily to accumulate inner strength and resolve, to fill and deepen our spiritual reservoirs. Make it your highest goal to cultivate your inner self. Set and keep a daily appointment with God. Withdraw from life's busyness to seek him in solitude.

All of this may mean getting up thirty minutes earlier, carving out forty minutes in the late morning or afternoon, or missing a television program in the evening. It is worth any sacrifice to spend time in his presence. No time spent with Christ is wasted time.

Nothing so cultivates the inner person and enriches our relationship with God as biblical meditation. Meditation is the process of pondering, musing, and reflecting upon God and his truth. In the process, our hearts are drawn to God, our thoughts are filled with his thoughts, and ultimately, our behavior becomes like Christ's.

Meditation is more than reading the Bible. It is musing upon it, rehearsing it prayerfully and thoughtfully. It is not swallowing Scripture whole, but chewing long and hard before digesting it. As a therapy for stress, meditation is often superior to medication. It is in prayerfully Christ-centered meditation that the peace of God is experienced and the inner life is bolstered to withstand the pressures of the outer life.

There is really no secret to meditation. All of us meditate. We may meditate on a novel, a TV program , a sermon, a song, a shopping list, a friend, or this morning's sidewalk sale. Right now you're meditating on this book. All of us meditate. The key to meditation is the *object* of meditation.

Biblical meditation focuses on God—his attributes (Psalm 48:9), his works (Psalm 77:11-12), and his Word (Psalm 119:15-16). As we meditate on him, we become increasingly like him.

We like to hear seven methods and five easy steps and three proven secrets to the Christian life. But there are no shortcuts to spirituality. There is no pill that makes us godly. We become more Christ-like only as we take pains to focus our gaze on Christ:

127

But we all, with unveiled face beholding as in a mirror the glory of the Lord, are being transformed into the same image from glory to glory (2 Corinthians 3:18, NASB).

FOOD FOR THOUGHT AND DISCUSSION

1. "All feelings of guilt are invalid and unhelpful." Do you agree or disagree? Why?

2. What do you learn about guilt in Psalm 32:3-5?

3. "Instead of accepting the atonement, some people try to repeat it." How and why do people do this? Give an example.

4. Have you ever had a case of the "I should haves" or "I shouldn't haves" when all you think about is what you've done wrong? If you were counseling her, what would you say to a Christian woman who is plagued by such thoughts?

5. If you are a Christian, according to God's Word, who are you? Describe yourself as God sees you.

6. Specifically, what can you do to focus more on developing biblical self-identity?

7. In a society that is preoccupied with appearances and image rather than character, what specifically can you do to cultivate your inner person?

1. Gordon MacDonald, *Ordering Your Private World* (Nashville: Thomas Nelson, 1984), p. 13.

8

ARE YOU MEANT TO BE WONDER-WIFE AND SUPER-MOM?

Families are mini-societies. Everything good in a society—love, loyalty, cohesiveness, and commitment—is at its best in the home. However, the same forces that cause war, labor disputes, political conflicts and protests in society are also daily at work in the home. These include different personalities, temperaments, perceptions and ideas, as well as sin, selfishness, narrow-mindedness, inflexibility, insensitivity, and poor communication. Put these together and they spell STRESS.

For those who strive to race through life as Wonder-Wife or Super-Mom the road is fraught with chuck holes and hairpin turns. We have no magic formulas that will make your impossible dream possible. But if you want to be a little better wife and a little better mom, and if you're willing to negotiate the road carefully with eyes wide open, this chapter is for you.

WORKING AT BEING A GOOD WIFE

Marriage is the heart of the home. A good marriage precedes good parenting, and no amount of good parenting compensates for a poor marriage.

If a woman expects her husband to meet all of her needs, she is setting herself up for all kinds of stress. Only God can ultimately meet our deepest needs of security and significance. To expect those needs to be met by another human being is to put him in the place of God, and to set up ourselves and him for disappointment.

Even if a husband could meet all his wife's needs (remember, he can't), he may die before she does (three out of four do). In other words, he not only lacks the omnipotence to meet all her needs, he is mortal. If your husband is *your* primary need-meeter, what will you do when he is gone? (God, on the other hand is never gone—"I am with you always.")

It is unfortunate but true that husbands may be unwilling even to meet those needs which they could meet. As many readers are painfully aware, a husband may neglect his wife, abuse her, become unfaithful or leave her. He may create deeper needs in her than he meets.

The woman addressed in 1 Peter 3:1-6 is married to an unbeliever or a spiritually insensitive believer. She is married, yet (like many Christian women) is spiritually single. Rather than sinking into despair or bitterness because her husband cannot or will not meet her needs, she is told to cultivate her relationship with the one true Need-meeter. As a result, she will live a life of purity with godly behavior that *may* win over her husband. Certainly she will not win him over by browbeating him for not meeting her needs.

Unfortunately, some women have been taught that 1 Peter 3 *guarantees* that their husbands will be won over if they do things right. But Scripture makes clear there is no such assurance (1 Corinthians 7:16).

We know women who have "tried" the 1 Peter 3 approach for several years, then given up because "it didn't work." But this passage is not a formula with a money-back guarantee. It is not something to "try," it is a lifestyle that is to be carried on regardless of whether a husband responds. For ultimately its highest purpose is not to win over a husband (though that is an exciting possible byproduct) but to please God.

Bringing your husband to Christ is a fine desire and a wonderful thing to pray for, but it is a poor goal. Why? Because no goal is good when it is beyond our control. It will only cause stress and make us feel guilty if we "fail" to do what was outside of our control in the first place. We need to live our lives for God. Then leave the results to him.

CONFLICT AND COMMUNICATION IN MARRIAGE

Conflict often stems from a failure to see the legitimacy of differences. The fact that another person—my neighbor, my friend, or my spouse—does and says things differently than I do is not bad. It is good. A society of clones, look-alikes, and work-alikes would be disastrous. A marriage of two identical people would make one of them unnecessary.

Conflict thrives on our differences, our quirks, our peculiar habits, right down to where we squeeze the toothpaste tube and which way we unroll the bathroom tissue. Like porcupines, we

133

jab, poke, and generally bug each other to the point of pain, and sometimes tears.

The worst part of conflict is not that it happens—that's inevitable—but what we allow it to do to us. Too easily we adopt the "I win, you lose" philosophy. In such a scenario egos are on the line, and while conflicts may eventually die of old age, they are not resolved. They won't be until the couple understands they are a team, and the truth is "If you win, I win and if you lose, I lose."

It is impossible to overestimate the importance to a marriage of deliberate, regular, and meaningful communication. Communication can prevent conflict, nip it in the bud, and foster its resolution.

Over the years, lack of communication and unresolved marital conflict will result in a self-building barrier of frightening proportions, as depicted in an anonymous poem, "The Wall." Read it carefully; if you're not communicating, the marriage it describes could some day be your own.

> Their wedding picture mocked them from the table, these two, whose minds no longer touched each other.
>
> They lived with such a heavy barricade between them that neither battering ram of words nor artilleries of touch could break it down.
>
> Somewhere between the oldest child's first tooth and the youngest daughter's graduation, they lost each other.
>
> Throughout the years, each slowly unraveled that tangled ball of string called self, and as they tugged at stubborn knots each hid his searching from the other.
>
> Sometimes she cried at night and begged the whispering darkness to tell her who she was.
>
> He lay beside her, snoring like a hibernating bear, unaware of her winter.

Once, after they had made love, he wanted to tell her how afraid he was of dying, but, fearing to show his naked soul, he spoke instead about the beauty of her breasts.

She took a course in modern art, trying to find herself in colors splashed upon a canvas, and complained to other women about men who were insensitive.

He climbed into a tomb called "the office," wrapped his mind in a shroud of paper figures and buried himself in customers.

Slowly, the wall between them rose, cemented by the mortar of indifference.

One day, reaching out to touch each other, they found a barrier they could not penetrate, and recoiling from the coldness of the stone, each retreated from the stranger on the other side.

For when love dies it is not in a moment of angry battle, nor when fiery bodies lose their heat.

It lies panting, exhausted, expiring at the bottom of a wall it could not scale.

Nothing is so good as a good marriage, and nothing is so bad as a bad one. It's worth every communicative effort on your part to preserve your marriage from "The Wall." No matter how hard it is to keep the wall from being built, it is always much harder to tear it down.

DEALING WITH SEXUAL PRESSURES IN MARRIAGE

Tremendous marital stress is often generated by the issues of sexual roles, the sexual relationship in marriage, and sexual temptation outside marriage.

In fact, when psychiatrist George Serban of New York University conducted a nationwide poll of a thousand married men and women from the ages of eighteen to sixty, he found *their greatest source of stress was the change in society's attitudes toward sex.*

This included both sexual permissiveness and the changing roles of the sexes.[1]

My book, *Christians in the Wake of the Sexual Revolution*, addresses the causes and effects of the sexual revolution and the challenges they present to Christian singles, couples, parents, the church, and society as a whole.[2] There are innumerable pressures put upon us by society, especially through the media, to abandon God's blueprint for sexual purity.

As a result of the impact of the sexual revolution, all of us need to be more aware of our own moral vulnerability. None of us is immune to sexual temptation. "If you think you are standing firm, be careful that you don't fall!" (1 Corinthians 10:12). In counseling I have talked with many women who never thought it possible, but have ended up having affairs. Why? Largely because *they never thought it possible*. Therefore, they failed to take proper precautions, and exposed themselves to temptations they should have carefully avoided.

It is not the desire for sex so much as the desire to meet inner needs that leads women into affairs. An uncultivated marriage has left them feeling dried up, unlovely, unlovable, and unloving. When they cross paths with a certain man at a certain time, they are flattered by his attention. They begin to take pride in their appearance, they cheer up for a while; for a brief time it appears they are coming out on top of their stress. But the bottom drops out—either when they realize what is happening, or, worse, after the affair materializes. If it does—as any woman knows who has been there—they are experiencing only the tip of the stress iceberg.

Sexual harmony in marriage is both a symbol and a potential cultivator of intimacy, as well as a guard against immorality (1 Corinthians 7:1-5). Despite what our self-proclaimed sexperts may tell us, sexual harmony is not primarily a matter of sexual technique or methodology. Many sex manuals, even some of the Christian variety, resemble a paint-by-the-numbers kit. It's better than nothing, perhaps, but the product may seem more like someone else's than your own. There's a place for some of these books, but sexual technique pales in importance to the cultivation of personal intimacy that comes through communicating and working through life's problems together.

Much stress in marriage generates from the vastly different sexual expectations—spoken or unspoken—of husbands and wives. Couples hesitate to discuss this matter, but it is in vital need of discussion, for more resentments breed in silence in this area than any other.

Some women need to recognize their clear biblical responsibility to regularly meet their husband's sexual needs (1 Corinthians 7:2-5). I counseled with a Christian woman who took great pride in the fact that she wouldn't allow her husband to touch her. She was shocked when I told her that sexually denying her husband was as gross a form of carnality as being unfaithful to him.

In the process of meeting your husband's sexual needs, you should try to communicate to him your own needs. Explain your need for romance, the right mood, the right environment, the importance of things such as warmth, cleanliness, a locked door—whatever makes you feel more free to express your love to him. Remember, however, that whether or not he meets your needs, you are responsible to try to meet his.

If you sense there may be a barrier between you and your husband in this area, I suggest you sit down with him early in the evening—before your minds and bodies are fried—and ask him "What do you think we can do to improve our sexual relationship?" When you are both working at sexual harmony, sex stops being a stress-producer and becomes a stress-reliever.[3]

SUPER-MOM AND MOTHER BURN-OUT

There's nothing quite like being a mom.

Moms and carpools are the backbone of the national frenzy of children's extracurricular activities (the theory seems to be that if every moment of a child's day is taken, he won't have time to misbehave). Take a mother of four children, ages nine to sixteen. In the last three years, she's had not only to get her children to school and back, she's contended with the practice and game schedules of swim team, diving team, water polo, grade school varsity football, high school JV football, rally, drill team, tennis . . . and the list goes on. The only things missing are hang gliding, deep sea fishing, and big game hunting—but Mom knows it's only a matter of time before these are included as well.

Nine-year-old Johnny isn't into more than three sports a year yet, but Mom is an aide at his school on Wednesday and is helping out on his Groundhog Day party on Friday—if she can get someone to pick up Jimmy from trumpet lessons and Jenny from her volleyball game. Of course, Mom will volunteer to drive the carpool Friday morning, even though she normally does it on Tuesday, since she has to be at Johnny's party anyway. Come to think of it, Jimmy will have to skip trumpet lessons Friday since he's running cross-country.

And team sports is just the beginning. There's stage band, orchestra, choir, yearbook, drama, speech club, computer club, chess club. Let's face it: Mom may be clubbed to death . . . if she doesn't drown in a car pool first.

Yes, there's nothing quite like being a mom. Who else but Mom (or "Hey, Mom" as she's often called), in a brief moment of madness, thinks she's finally going to get a long uninterrupted bath (the last one was two years ago), only to hear her five-year-old press his mouth up to the door and ask, "Mommy, do slugs stain the carpet?" Who else is told by her teenage daughter (the one with the phone growing out her ear), "Everyone else has a horse and their ears pierced and goes to Hawaii with a friend, so why can't I?" Who else gets to watch her teenage son inhale five sandwiches and a gallon of milk then say, "I'm starved—isn't there *anything* to eat?"

Being a mother is lots of fun . . . as long as you pace yourself and maintain your sense of humor. Those who don't are doomed to burnout.

Burnout is most common in the helping professions, such as counseling, nursing, teaching and pastoring. But the ultimate helping profession is mothering. Are you in danger of mother burnout?

The following quiz is a slightly adapted version of one developed by Dr. Joseph Procaccini, author of *Parent Burnout*.[4] Answer each question yes or no, then score yourself based on the point values that follow the quiz:

Yes No 1. Do you think your family couldn't get along without you?

Yes No 2. Do you tend to compare yourself unfavorably to other mothers?

Yes No 3. When your children act up, do your "little slaps" sometimes get harder than they should?

Yes No 4. Would you consider it a compliment if someone called you a "Super-Mom?"

Yes No 5. Are you cross, impatient, and on edge? If your child drops a dish, do you explode?

Yes No 6. Does it seem to you that being a mother is often like being on a treadmill—you work hard but go nowhere?

Yes No 7. At the end of a day with your children, do you feel physically and psychologically drained?

Yes No 8. Do you feel that all your kids do is take, take, take, while expecting you to give and keep on giving?

Yes No 9. Do you find yourself forgetting routine things, like whether you unplugged the coffee pot or where you parked the car?

Yes No 10. Do you ever have the feeling that your kids are out to get you?

Yes No 11. Do you ever daydream about just walking out on your family and never coming back?

Yes No 12. Do you feel very embarrassed when your children act up in front of other adults?

Yes No 13. Do you feel very guilty when you lose your patience or fail as a mother?

Yes No 14. Do you feel totally responsible for the way your children are turning out?

Yes No 15. If you and your children disagree, do you feel powerless to make them do things your way?

To score yourself, enter in the spaces below the point values that appear in parenthesis alongside each question to which you've answered "yes." ("No" answers always count as zero.) Then, add them all up to get your score. (For example, if you answered "yes" to only questions 2 and 8, your score would be

17.) Your score will be somewhere between 0 and 100. The higher it is, the closer you are to mother burnout.

Scoring: Points for "yes" answers only.

1. (3 points)		9. (3 points)
2. (7 points)		10. (10 points)
3. (10 points)		11. (10 points)
4. (3 points)		12. (5 points)
5. (10 points)		13. (5 points)
6. (7 points)		14. (3 points)
7. (7 points)		15. (7 points)
8. (10 points)		

Total _____

If your total is 20 or below, you are at no immediate risk of burnout. According to Dr. Procaccini, about 20 percent of U.S. mothers fall into this category.

A score of 21-53 means you are simmering. You are on the verge of trouble and need to take preventive action. You need to cut back on some of your demands on yourself and try to rest more, exercise more, and do more things you enjoy.

If your score falls between 54-86, you are at the boiling point. You need to make some immediate and substantial changes.

If your score is over 86, you are boiling over. Dr. Procaccini says that 13 percent of mothers are in this category. If you are, you need help. See a counseling pastor or a professional Christian counselor as soon as possible.

WHY DO MOMS BURN OUT?

Burnout is most common among mothers with high standards for themselves and their children. Christian mothers often have the highest standards of any. The Christian mom reads the books, listens to the radio programs, goes to the seminars, and learns how to be the perfect mother and how to raise perfect kids. When she and they fall short of perfection, she takes it on the chin.

She feels guilty when she loses patience with the children. Yet she sanctimoniously says "no" to any activity that takes her away from the kids for the day or the weekend when, in fact, that is exactly what she and they desperately need. Mom may worry that the children won't get along well staying with someone else (of course, the only way they'll learn is by doing it, and when they do it periodically they'll usually love it). But her secret fear may be that her children will do fine without her. Super-Mom wants and needs to be needed and she will be— even if it kills her and her children.

Super-Mom sets herself and her children up for failure. She unwittingly breeds insecurity by making everything a big deal. It bothers her that Bobby got a *C* in math or that Barbie has to repeat her beginning swimming class because she couldn't do her front floats. She sees her child's immaturity as something bad instead of something natural. Super-Mom pressures her children to grow up too fast. David Elkind has addressed this rampant social problem in his excellent book *The Hurried Child*.[5] There is a serious danger in imposing adult standards of performance on those who—by definition of the word *children*—are not adults.

The hurried child is hurried by the hurried mom. She's like the circus plate spinner constantly gyrating back and forth, this way and that, to keep all the plates spinning. A moment's rest, one missed swivel, and something will crash—maybe even her image of Super-Mom.

Super-Mom doesn't have time to smile and giggle and play light-heartedly with the children—she's too busy driving car pools, planning parties, arranging soccer lessons, making Halloween costumes and baking brownies for the Scouts party. She's so busy working for her kids she has no time to give them what they need most—herself. Your children will remember a lot less about what you did *for* them than what you did *with* them. They don't care whether you're nominated Mother of the Year. They just want *you*.

Being your child's mother is more important than being his social coordinator, activities director, and servant. And that means being the most content, relaxed, and balanced mother you can be.

One Saturday morning when our daughters were six and four, Nanci and I were planning to sleep in till about 8:00 A.M. At 7:30 Angie, our four-year-old, got up from watching cartoons, came into our bedroom, stood about five inches away from Nanci's ear, and in a mournful voice said these exact words (I wrote them down): "Mommy, why are you laying in bed sleeping when you should be getting breakfast for your two little girls?"

Kids know just how to turn the knife in your guilt complex. We had to be ready to point out that at six and four they were perfectly capable of picking up a box of cereal and a carton of milk that one Saturday morning. Mothers who always do everything for their children invite manipulation, and not only spoil their children but burn themselves out.

EXCELLENCE OR FAITHFULNESS?

"Too many people have a piece of me," Jane lamented. "I can't give them what I don't have, and I just don't have anything left."

Jane was experiencing job saturation. She was totally devoted to motherhood, the church, social action, and every good cause imaginable. In her case it stemmed from unrealistic expectations. Jane was the type of woman who could be told, "Rome wasn't built in a day," and would respond, "That's because I wasn't in charge of the project."

We assured Jane she didn't have to try to be what she wasn't—the fourth member of the trinity or vice-president in charge of the galaxy. She didn't have to save the whole world because that was Jesus' job, not hers. Her family would still love her even if she didn't win the Nobel Peace Prize this year.

Many women say to themselves, "I must do everything well." The implication of this belief is that they must be the world's best mother, a gourmet cook, the perfect hostess, have a spotless home, and be a ravishing beauty queen. Realistically this is just not possible. If you know someone who seems to be all these things, she's probably going to someone like me for counseling, saying, "I can't take it anymore."

We have a confession to make—we're sick and tired of hearing so much about the importance of excellence in all things. While we're all for excellence, and all of us should strive for it in some areas, it is impossible for any of us to be excellent in everything. Pretending we can be or should be just sets us up for the crash.

Neither Nanci nor I is an excellent runner, and never will be, but that doesn't mean we have no business running. We aren't art critics and can't draw worth anything, but that doesn't stop us from drawing pictures for our girls. I am a poor ice skater, but I can go ice-skating with our family and still have a blast (the fact that I'm so bad is half the fun). Like you, both of us can do a few things with excellence, but it would lay an unbearable weight on us if we thought we had to be excellent in everything.

Christ has called us not to excellence in all things but to *faithfulness* in all things (1 Corinthians 4:2). Every man I know would much rather be married to a faithful woman who's a fair cook, a competent housekeeper, a good mom, and a decent wife than a woman whose devotion to excellence in all things leaves her strung-out, uptight, and intolerant of herself and her family.

So while you're doing a few excellent things today, relax and do some strictly average ones, maybe even a few below average. In fact, why don't you find something you do poorly, and do it with gusto. It will do your heart good!

One more suggestion along the same line: come to grips with Murphy's Laws of Motherhood. If anything can go wrong, it will. Nothing is as easy as it looks. Everything takes longer than you think. Every solution breeds new problems. A phone rings the moment you step in the bath. There's always an easier way to do it, but you never find out until it's done. It always costs less somewhere else, but no one tells you until after you buy it (and then they won't stop telling you).

COMPARISON AND PEOPLE-PLEASING

Much perfectionism is really unspoken competition stemming from comparison. One of Nanci's closest friends has an oven that is cleaner than the hospital's intensive care unit. If a cockroach came within ten feet of her house it would die from the sheer sterility of the environment.

As their friendship developed, Nanci started feeling she needed to step up her own housework. But then she realized that her friend didn't expect this of her (if she did, she wouldn't have been a friend, right?). And she realized, too, that her friend's situation was different. She didn't have small children anymore. She not only had more time to do the housework, but there was no one following her around all day to undo it. Besides, people are different. Nanci excelled in some areas, her friend in others.

Young mothers do each other a major disservice when they invite one another over to their homes. When a friend is coming over, they clear the living room and cram the toys, books, blankets and stuffed animals into the bedroom, lean on the door, and bend it till it latches. As a result, the living room looks clean to the unsuspecting other mother.

So this other young mother goes home with a complex, saying to herself, "Something must be wrong with me—she has kids and her house is always neat." Of course, all her friends think her house is always neat too, because she pulls the same "dump the toys in the bedroom" trick when she hears their approaching hoofbeats.

Why can't we just be honest with each other and take some of the pressure off?

WORKING TWO JOBS

All the pressures we've described apply to the woman who works that full-time unsalaried job known as "Justa Housewife." But what about the millions of mothers who are also working outside the home, many of them full-time?

It is usually financially necessary for single mothers to work outside the home, though some manage to generate sufficient income working at home. We are not addressing single moms here. God understands the dilemma of the single mom and offers her special grace. In fact, some of the best moms we know are single. The rest of us need to reach out and help them any way we can, to maximize the time they do have with their children.

However, many mothers who work long hours outside the home do not have to, and they may be setting themselves up for a crash. Do you remember the television commercial with the female executive, briefcase in hand, wearing a sharp business suit, looking like a million bucks? Then, like a perpetual motion machine straight from a beauty parlor, she takes over her job in the home. The song croons, "I can bring home the bacon, fry it up in a pan, and never let you forget you're a man." This, apparently, is "having it all" (at least it's *doing* it all). Today's ideal woman is an aggressive breadwinner, immaculate housekeeper, master chef, and relentless sexpot all rolled up in one. And women are told they can actually sustain this level of responsibility without cracking up!

But Christian women who try to live out both full-time roles—homemaker and breadwinner—must ask themselves honestly if their primary scriptural calling—"to love [take care of] their husbands and children" and "to be busy at home" (Titus 2:4, 5)—is being hindered through their outside work.

Does working twenty or thirty or forty hours a week outside the home contribute to or take away from the quantity and quality of time a woman has with her family? Does it result in more or less involvement in their lives, increased or decreased opportunity to be with them, listen to them, minister to them, keep her finger on their pulses?

Even the mother whose children are in school must ask herself if she can really focus on them and her husband in the evenings, or if household duties (that could have been done during the day if she was home), other interests, and fatigue will distract her from them.

The feminist movement may have given wives and mothers lots of new jobs, but it hasn't taken away their old ones. The result? Lots of stressed-out women trying to do two or more full-time jobs.

The tragedy is that many women seek self-fulfillment outside the home because they've been indoctrinated into believing they cannot find such fulfillment inside the home. Marian told us, "I want to get out in the working world, away from diapers and dishes, where I can do something that really counts." Counts in whose eyes and for how long?

Women who once believed the maxim "The hand that rocks the cradle rules the world" are now rubbing shoulders with the movers and shakers in Fortune 500 companies, and have become content to let the day care centers rule the world. Tragically, many of them fail to consider that what is actually being moved and shaken in that exciting world of business (and busyness) may amount, in the eyes of eternity, to a hill of beans.

We firmly believe that there are many business world movers and shakers whose lifetime accomplishments will pale compared to those of "Justa Housewife" who stayed home and loved her husband and took care of her children in a host of ways, many of them routine and mundane. Such a woman is a mover and shaker of her family, and her work at home will bear fruit in them—and her—in ways no paycheck can equal.

Most American families do not need more money. They need to learn how to manage the money they have. Until they do, having more money will just mean having more to mismanage. For most families who cannot live on one paycheck, expenditures will always rise to meet income at any level. Furthermore, studies show the second income is always far less than it appears to be. Much of it is lost in higher taxes and the costs of transportation, eating lunches out, expensive clothes, child care, and many other hidden expenses. But the greatest hidden cost is to the family who needs a full-time mother infinitely more than a court club membership, an RV, and a hot tub on the patio. In the interests of a "higher standard of living" too many Christian women sacrifice what Scripture says is a higher standard of life.

We're not saying no woman should work outside the home. We're simply encouraging married women whose husbands work and whose children are not yet grown to evaluate whether they really *need* to work outside the home, and if so, how much. Is it worth the added stress and the knowledge deep inside that despite all the propaganda to the contrary, you cannot give yourself fully to two full-time jobs?

GETTING HELP

Many moms know how to give but not how to receive. Jesus said, "It is more blessed to give than to receive" (Acts 20:35). Don't rob your loved ones of the blessing of giving to you. Don't be a poor receiver.

Two pieces of advice for the many women who need more help from their families:

1. Ask for help nicely.

2. Accept help graciously.

Communicate with your family. Admit you're not Superwoman. Ask your husband's help. Rather than chiding him for what he hasn't done, commend him for what he has, and ask if he can do even more. Teach your children to do chores, and delegate responsibility to them. This isn't just to help you, it's to help them become responsible people. Show your family specific ways they can help, like putting away cereal boxes, picking up dishes from the table and rinsing them off, putting all dirty clothes in the hamper, keeping fingers off mirrors, etc. Be specific, positive, and as considerate of them as you would like them to be of you.

Try to do all this before your condition deteriorates to a breakdown or you succumb to a "poor me" mentality or to a seething resentment that results in bitter outbursts and demands, threats and ultimatums ("Start doing your part or I'm leaving home"). This means you must continually evaluate your stress level and keep your finger on your emotional pulse.

Every woman has the right to expect help from her family. Likewise every family has a right to expect she will express her needs openly, honestly, and graciously—whenever possible, *before* she hits the breaking point.

FOOD FOR THOUGHT AND DISCUSSION

1. Do you think most people experience more or less stress in their family relationships than in other relationships? Why?

2. What happens when one marriage partner expects the other to meet most or all of his/her needs?

3. Remember the poem "The Wall"? After rereading it, what parts of it make an impression on you?

4. What pressures has the sexual revolution brought on marriages today? What can a married woman do to enhance her sexual relationship with her husband and to maintain her purity? How can single women cultivate and guard their sexual purity?

5. How did you do on the "Mother Burnout" test? Were you surprised? Why or why not?

6. Why do Christian moms burn out? What can they do to prevent it?

7. "God has called us to faithfulness in all things, not excellence in all things." Do you agree or disagree? Explain.

8. What good things have come from the feminist movement? What bad things have come from it? Which do you think outweighs the other, the good or the bad?

9. "Most single women and some married women need to work outside the home, but if at all possible mothers should not do so when their children are young." Agree or disagree? If you can, defend your answer from Scripture.

1. Claudia Wallis, "Stress: Can We Cope?" *Time*, 6 June 1983, p. 48.
2. Randy C. Alcorn, *Christians in the Wake of the Sexual Revolution* (Portland, Ore.: Multnomah Press, 1985).
3. The subject of sex roles is touched on at a few points in this book, but is generally beyond its scope. I recommend Ronald and Beverly Allen's fine book, *Liberated Traditionalism* (Portland, Ore.: Multnomah Press, 1985).
4. Joseph Procaccini and Mark Kiefaber, *Parent Burnout* (New York: Doubleday, 1983).
5. David Elkind, *The Hurried Child: Growing Up Too Fast Too Soon* (Reading, Mass.: Addison-Wesley, 1981).

MANAGING YOUR TIME AND TASKS BEFORE THEY MANAGE YOU

"**D**ost thou love life? Then do not squander time, for that is the stuff which life is made of."

Over three thousand years before Benjamin Franklin said those words, Moses said these:

Teach us to number our days aright,
　　that we may gain a heart of wisdom (Psalm 90:12).

The New Testament speaks the same message: "Redeem the time," or "Make the most of every opportunity" (Colossians 4:5).

Time management is life management. But we don't need to save time in order to fill it up with more responsibilities. Rather, we need to manage our lives better so we may take more time to enjoy the Lord, our families, our church, our neighbors, and all the important people and opportunities of life that too often get buried beneath our busyness.

THE URGENT VS. THE IMPORTANT

The first and greatest time management principle is truly a liberating one: *In the final analysis, I have only one thing to do.* Does this principle sound strange? It comes straight from the mouth of Jesus. Do you remember when the two sisters from Bethany, Martha and Mary, gave a dinner party for Jesus and his disciples in their home? Martha was busily doing dozens of things that "needed to be done"—or so she told herself. Mary, meanwhile, was taking the opportunity to sit at Jesus' feet and enjoy his company.

Martha got uptight because there was so much to do and so little time. She finally blurted out to Jesus her resentment toward Mary for spending the time with him instead of helping her serve the meal. We can imagine Jesus gently placing his hand on Martha's shoulder as he said:

Martha, Martha, you are worried and upset about many things, but only one thing is needed. Mary has chosen what is better, and it will not be taken away from her (Luke 10:41-42).

The passage says Mary chose "what is better" or literally, "the better portion." The reference is to food, and it sets up an interesting contrast. While Martha devoted herself to preparing physical food, Mary devoted herself to receiving spiritual food. She was a hungry soul, single-mindedly devoted to the spiritual meal served by Jesus.

The time we spend with God determines the direction and the quality of all the rest of our time. Because of this, the more pressures we face, the more time we need to spend with God in order to face them properly. That's why Martin Luther did what at first glance seems senseless—on days when he had more to do he spent more time in prayer.

Robert Hummell's *The Tyranny of the Urgent* reminds us we must learn to discern between the urgent and the truly important.[1] Serving the guests seemed much more urgent to Martha than listening to Jesus. But what she failed to realize was that it was also far less important.

Every woman's day is filled with things that are urgent—appointments, housework, homework, phone calls, car pools, shopping. *If I don't do the wash tonight, there'll be no clean clothes tomorrow. If I don't study, I'll fail tomorrow's final exam.* All of us feel the urgency. But if we don't spend time with the Lord or read to our children or call our parents, life goes on. These things are not emergencies. In neglecting them we don't neglect something urgent. We neglect something important.

In the long run, doing the urgent at the expense of the important always catches up with us. This is especially true with our children, as Erma Bombeck captures so well in her article "There Wasn't Time":

> When I was young, Mama was going to read me a story and I was going to turn the pages and pretend I could read. But she had to wax the bathroom and there wasn't time.

> When I was young, Daddy was going to come to school and watch me in a play. I was the fourth wise man (in case one of the three got sick), but he was having his car tuned and there was no time.

When I was young, Grandma and Granddad were going to come for Christmas to see the expression on my face when I got my first bike, but Grandma didn't know who she could get to feed the dogs and Granddad didn't like the cold weather and, besides, they didn't have the time.

When I was older, Dad and I were going fishing one weekend, just the two of us, and we were going to pitch a tent and fry fish with the heads on them. But at the last minute he had to fertilize the garden and there wasn't time.

When I was older, the whole family was always going to pose together for our Christmas card. But my brother had ball practice, my sister had her hair up, Dad was watching the Colts and Mom had to mop the kitchen. There wasn't time.

When I grew up and left home to be married, I was going to sit down with Mom and Dad and tell them I loved them and would miss them. But Hank (he was our best man and a real clown) was honking the horn in front of the house, so there wasn't time.[2]

STEPS TO TIME MANAGEMENT

Nanci and I sit down periodically to take stock of what we are doing with our lives, and we have often discovered that our real priorities (demonstrated in how we spend our time) haven't reflected our ideal priorities (how we believe our time is best spent).

We suggest you try this kind of evaluation yourself by making a list of all your daily and weekly activities. Here are some things to include (add others of your own):

devotions	eating	exercise
writing letters	school	study
relaxation	sleep/naps	housework
yard/garden	church work	volunteer work
shopping	driving	church activities

daily routine:	watching TV	husband
bathing	reading	children
getting dressed	phone calls	parents/in-laws
doing makeup	hobbies	friends
job/career		

For a week or two, keep track of how much time you spend on each of these, and write down the total. Once you've determined how you spend your time, the next step is deciding how you *want* to spend your time. Techniques to save time are ultimately useless until you've decided what you want to do with the time you've saved. Time that is saved but uncommitted somehow manages to disappear.

If you've determined how much time you spend on the above and other things, go back and put the letter "M" for "more" next to the things you want or need to do more, the letter "L" for "less" by those you want or need to do less. Cross out the things you can afford not to do, add things you presently aren't doing but want to do.

Note that since you are presently using all the time you have, *in order to add anything, something must go.* If you add choir practice on Tuesday nights, it must come from laundry, family, exercise, devotions, sleeping, television, phone calls or somewhere. Remember, time is like money—spend it on one thing and you can't spend it on another. So get the best value for your time. Spend it wisely—but don't overspend.

PLAN HOW YOU USE YOUR TIME

We all need free time to relax, but many of us never get it because we have no handle on our schedules. Unbudgeted time fritters away like unbudgeted money. When you have a schedule book you can block out time for all your major priorities and tasks. Write them all down and look over your calendar daily. This way you know what's coming (most of life's surprises really aren't that fun!). Don't say "yes" to anything until you've checked your calendar.

When Donna asks you to go shopping all day Thursday don't just say "yes." Look at your calendar. Ah ha, company's coming over Thursday night. So if you're going to go shopping all day Thursday you'd better get the house in order and plan your Thursday's dinner on Wednesday. Uh oh, you see on your calendar you're working as a teacher's aide at the school Wednesday, and that night is your Bible study group. Come to think of it, better tell Donna you can shop with her Friday, but not Thursday (or maybe not at all if you're going to be too tired from Thursday).

Whether single, married, or employed in or out of the home, a schedule book can help lessen your stress. Executives can't live without them. You have as much to do as an executive, and you probably don't have a secretary to remind you of things or a receptionist to screen your calls. So write out your schedule—and not on the back of junk mail envelopes.

GUIDELINES FOR TIME MANAGEMENT

Make a daily list and follow it one task at a time. Write down everything you think you can and should accomplish today—lists kept "in your head" get lost there.

You can make your list in the morning or the night before. List your responsibilities in consecutive order. You may want to put an asterisk (*) by those things that absolutely must be done today. Start tomorrow's list with what you didn't get done today.

Don't start writing a letter, then move to folding clothes, then begin a batch of cookies, then start to vacuum, then make a phone call. This is what leaves you at the end of the day with laundry baskets in the bedroom, a vacuum in the living room, and an unfinished letter (stained with cookie dough) on the kitchen table.

Enlist help. Don't be afraid to delegate or ask a friend for help. Do you have ten calls to make related to the women's meeting Tuesday? Call Lucy who started coming a few weeks ago and hasn't gotten involved yet. Ask her if she can make five of the calls for you. If your schedule is really tight, ask someone else to make the other five.

One of our biggest mistakes is thinking we must do everything ourselves. The belief that "To do it right I have to do it myself" has been the motto of many right up to the day they're admitted to the hospital with a nervous breakdown.

Share the load! "Carry each other's burdens, and in this way you will fulfill the law of Christ" (Galatians 6:2). The same principle applies to our responsibilities. In order to be bearing one another's responsibilities, we also must be sharing our own responsibilities with others. Doing so not only releases us, it gets others involved who need to be. It helps them to become ministers instead of spectators.

When possible, avoid or prevent interruptions. Mothers, one of the most important things you can teach your children—and you can begin when they are toddlers—is to respect your time. When the girls were two and four, Nanci taught them to have their own quiet time everyday while she had hers. They flipped through picture books or listened to records and learned not to interrupt her. Not only was it great for her, it had a positive quieting effect on them.

Tasks that should take thirty minutes take hours when we stop to answer the phone. Why not unplug the phone for thirty minutes? Some people define "emergency" as any time they want to talk with you—there are few true emergencies. Learn to deal with people who would monopolize your time. If you can't afford to talk for an hour, tell Lisa right up front "I'm working on a project—I can either talk to you five minutes now or call you back around 3:00."

Learn to politely stop telephone and door to door salesmen if you're uninterested. Since they are trained to talk for half an hour without stopping to breathe, this will require that you interrupt them.

Always plan for the unplanned. No matter how hard you try to eliminate the unexpected, it will be impossible to have 100 percent success. Whether you allow time for these things or not, they will come. We have stopped planning back to back events assuming everything will go smoothly, programs will end on time, and traffic will be flowing. If something should take an hour, we block out at least an hour and a half in our schedule books. Prepare in order to avoid frustration—or prepare to be frustrated.

Plan efficiently. Before driving six miles to the wallpaper store to see if they have your order in yet, use the phone.

Nanci and I try to consolidate our trips. We don't drive to the bookstore today when we know that tomorrow we're picking up fish at the market next door to the bookstore. Neither do we make special jaunts to the quickie-mart for nice-but- nonessentials like sour cream or croutons. We've discovered that the "I can always run out and get it" mentality costs us more time and money and energy than we realized.

Mobility has its advantages, but it can also be a curse. When our great grandmothers traveled to town only once a month, they had to buy everything and see everything in that trip. Then they had twenty-nine days uncluttered by trips here and there. Pretend you live a hundred miles from the nearest store, and plan your meals at least a week, and maybe two weeks or a month in advance.

Favor simplicity over complexity. Meals can be delicious and nutritious without being elaborate. It doesn't take a five course meal to please a family.

Choose a hairstyle that's nice but doesn't demand an extra thirty minutes each day. If you're planting a garden because you enjoy gardening, great. If it's going to become a hassle for you, weigh the actual money you save (usually much less than you think) against the number of hours you'll have to invest in the garden.

Think strategically. Make decisions not just on the basis of what looks good or seems good, but on how much of your time it will demand.

Be punctual. A great deal of stress can be saved by arriving places on time. Arriving late starts everything on the wrong foot. It shows poor planning and a low regard for the people or event you're going to. It often leaves you embarrassed and irritable, and frequently triggers a family fight on the way there (how many times have you entered a worship service straight from the battle zone?).

The key to punctuality is getting up earlier, having meals earlier, getting dressed earlier, doing everything earlier—including going to bed earlier. Allow at least thirty minutes and preferably an hour for unforeseen delays.

The magic of getting the family to church and the kids to school on time is nothing more than mind over mattress. We've determined to avoid going out on Saturday nights, because it makes Sunday morning so much more pleasant when we've stayed home and gone to bed at a reasonable hour.

Of course, everyone is late occasionally. When you are, accept that fact and try to relax. Being uptight can't help a thing, but it can and will hurt. One other thought about being punctual—it usually gives you a few minutes of privacy.

Match your tasks to your energy levels. For many of us, morning is when energy is at its peak and the mind is sharpest. If possible, give that time to your Bible study and prayer. Then balance the checkbook and do other things that require extra thought or energy.

Save trips outside the house for the afternoon. The stimulation of the grocery store will help you to keep moving. Often phone calls can be made in the afternoon as well. If you spend your morning outside the home or on the phone and don't hit your difficult tasks till the afternoon, inevitably they won't get done or they won't get done well.

THE PERILS OF PROCRASTINATION

Procrastination is putting off till tomorrow what can and should be done today. It is perhaps the most common form of self-induced stress.

Procrastination shows itself in many forms. When there's an important job to be done, usually with a deadline, we may fritter away our time in any number of self-indulgences—a big meal, a long nap, an extra cup of coffee, a drive, shopping, reading, daydreaming, a needless phone call or, most common of all, watching television. Meanwhile what we need to get done—maybe housework or Bible study preparation or grading a stack of school papers—hangs over our head.

Procrastination stems from disliking the task, being indifferent toward the task, or being frightened or threatened by the

. Sometimes there is so much to do that we don't know where to begin. So we don't.

How *Do* You Get Started?

Get things in order. When my card files are disorganized and my word processor is buried in books and magazines and pieces of paper with notes on them, I don't want to start writing. When everything's in order, it invites me to go to work.

If you're putting off balancing the checkbook, maybe it's because the checkbook is a mess. You've cut corners and your system stinks. Why not change it? An orderly checkbook invites your attention. The other kind invites procrastination—and eventual disaster.

Do the least desirable task first. Then move on to the others you like. If you save the undesirable task for later you'll run out of resolve and energy. And the stress of the undone job will hang over you until you do it anyway.

Divide and conquer. If you must read a hundred pages for a class by Friday afternoon and it's already Tuesday morning, divide by the four days you have left and read twenty-five pages today. Any big task becomes manageable when you break it up into smaller ones.

Cut off your escape routes. If you have a household project to do, turn off the TV—put it in a closet if you can, unplug the phone, have your husband or roommate hide your car keys, and get to work. Often the hardest part is just starting.

Give yourself rewards for finishing the task or phases of the task. Your reward might be a treat or a walk or a nap or an hour reading a favorite book or magazine.

Often, though, finishing is its own best reward. There is no feeling quite so good as having the house ready for company a day in advance, finishing a term paper or preparation for a talk several days or a week in advance, or having your Christmas shopping done in October.

So, if you're going to put off anything, put off procrastinating.

160

THE FINE ART OF SELECTION

More basic than planning your days is planning your life. Life consists largely of selection—choosing one alternative over another. Those things we choose are our priorities.

Deciding "I'll read the Bible and pray when I can find the time" is like saying "I'll give to God's work when I can find the money." There are an infinite number of things on which both time and money can be spent. Without a careful plan and self-discipline, expenditures always rise to meet income. Living beyond your means of time—trying to spend time that you don't have—is courting disaster.

The hardest lesson we've learned in the last ten years is this: life is full of good, worthwhile, and meaningful organizations, causes, and ministry opportunities—the vast majority of which we cannot and should not be involved with!

It is not sufficient that something be good or important. It must be the best and most important for me. Why? For the same reason that if I have a hundred dollars to spend on groceries this month, I should buy bread and milk and fruit and vegetables, not steaks and chips and expensive ready-made foods. Most good things I will never be able to do. If I try to do all or most or even a lot of them, I'll burn out and end up dropping out of half of them and doing the rest poorly.

We sometimes mistake religious activity and Christian busyness for true spirituality, failing to realize that overcommitment is no more honoring to God than undercommitment. In our relentless pursuit of spiritual success, we drag ourselves through a dizzy, busy, barren life. Our unspoken motto seems to be "Weariness is next to godliness."

Michelle was a real servant in her church, always available to organize a shower, stuff bulletins, sell banquet tickets, and help with the women's retreat. Some Sundays Michelle never made it to worship service because she taught Sunday school one hour and filled in for an absent nursery worker the next. Finally, she burnt out and left the church.

In the next two months you may be asked to host a luncheon, collect for the American Cancer Society, teach a class, lead a discussion group, work in the church nursery, be a room mother, run a booth at the carnival, serve punch at a wedding, picket an abortion clinic, be a teacher's aide, cook for the high school group camp-out, and go on the women's retreat. Very likely it is God's will for you to do a few of these good things. But *all* of them?

Consider making it a policy never to say "yes" to anything until you've thought and prayed about it for one week. Even if someone needs an answer today, tell them you'll call them back in a few hours. Don't impulsively say "Yes" or you will feel—and be—out-of-control.

(Of course, there's also the woman who always says "No" to everything and needs to learn to say "Yes." Be sure you say "Yes" enough to get your exercise, and "no" enough to get your rest.)

THE TYRANNY OF SELF-FULFILLMENT

What you say "Yes" to will depend on your values. Do your values center on spiritual growth, family relationships, intellectual development, using your gifts and skills, personal enrichment, self-expression, impact on others, pleasing people, recognition, fun, money, possessions?

Many books on goals and decision-making focus on values clarification. Most of us, however, are also in need of values *purification*. We need to take a good hard look not only at what we are doing but why we are doing it. We need to lay out our schedule books at the feet of Christ and ask him, "Lord, what would you have me do—and not do?"

In the name of self-fulfillment many women are joining this group and taking that class and, as we saw in the last chapter, adding one full-time job to another (that of being wife and mother). By all means take an art class or join a reading group if it enriches you. But choose carefully and know where to draw the line, or you'll be stressed. Judith Viorst captures this dilemma beautifully in her book *How Did I Get to Be Forty and Other Atrocities*:

I've finished six pillows in Needlepoint,
And I'm reading Jane Austen and Kant,
And I'm up to the pork with black beans in Advanced
  Chinese Cooking.
I don't have to struggle to find myself
For I already know what I want.
I want to be healthy and wise and extremely
  good-looking.

I'm learning new glazes in Pottery Class,
And I'm playing new chords in Guitar.
And in Yoga I'm starting to master the lotus position.
I don't have to ponder priorities
For I already know what they are:
To be good-looking, healthy, and wise.
And adored in addition.

I'm improving my serve with a tennis pro,
And I'm practicing verb forms in Greek,
And in Primal Scream Therapy all my frustrations
  are vented.
I don't have to ask what I'm searching for
Since I already know that I seek
To be good-looking, healthy, and wise.
And adored.
And contented.

I've bloomed in Organic Gardening,
And in Dance I have tightened my thighs,
And in Consciousness Raising there's no one
  around who can top me.
And I'm working all day and I'm working all night
To be good-looking, healthy, and wise.
And adored.
And contented.
And brave.
And well-read.
And a marvelous hostess,
And bilingual,
Athletic,
Artistic . . .
Won't someone please stop me?[3]

FOOD FOR THOUGHT AND DISCUSSION

1. "In the final analysis I have only one thing to do." What does this principle refer to in the context of Luke 10:38-42? How can we apply it?

2. What is "the tyranny of the urgent"? What is important and what is urgent, and how can we tell the difference?

3. If you made a list of your activities and how you spend your time, were you surprised or dissatisfied at how much or how little time you spend on certain things or people? In what way?

4. What would you like to spend more time doing?

5. What would you like to spend less time doing?

6. Are you satisfied with the way you have organized your life and your tasks? Why or why not?

7. How does procrastination produce stress? How can we avoid procrastination?

8. What's the problem with being the kind of person who always says "no"? What's the problem with being the kind that always says "yes"? Do you tend to be one or the other? What's the key to changing?

1. Robert Hummell, *The Tyranny of the Urgent* (Downer's Grove, Ill.: Inter-Varsity Press).

2. Erma Bombeck, "There Wasn't Time," *Newsday*, 17 November 1971.

3. Judith Viorst, *How Did I Get to be Forty and Other Atrocities* (New York: Simon & Schuster, 1973), p. 45.

10

HOW EXERCISING RIGHT RELIEVES STRESS

Going through life with a needlessly unfit body is like leaving on vacation with bad brakes, bald tires, and a six-cylinder engine running on three cylinders. The car might get you out of town if you're lucky, but not much further. Meanwhile, you're going to have a rough ride. An unfit body may take you a ways down the road of life, but not nearly as far or as smoothly as it would have with just thirty minutes of daily maintenance.

For an investment of less than 5 percent of our time, we can see a return of 100 percent in the quality and perhaps even the longevity of our life.

We've all heard that exercise is good for us. Still, many of us don't understand why exercise is so critical and how it can improve our lives. Even if you do understand, you've likely ignored or rationalized your own lack of consistent exercise. You may have procrastinated beginning an exercise program, or you may have begun one—or several—only to give it up at the first rain, cough, sore muscle or busy time of the year.

You may also be one of the many who *do* exercise regularly, thinking they are receiving maximum benefits when they really aren't. For the truth is that all exercises are *not* created equal.

Exercise physiologists have discovered that there is a specific kind of exercise—*aerobic* exercise—that can not only lengthen our life, but in many cases dramatically improve our health, our sense of well-being, and our ability to handle stress.

AEROBIC EXERCISE AND FAT REDUCTION

A primary stress-relieving benefit of aerobic exercise is its ability to significantly reduce and control body fat. To understand the far-reaching implications of this, we must understand the problem with excess body fat.

An overfat body places tremendous stress on the skeletal-muscular system, as well as the heart, lungs and other major organs. If a person is overfat, the likelihood of heart disease, heart attack, stroke, Type II diabetes, and most other diseases is significantly increased. The risk level in undergoing surgery, even routine surgery, escalates. If a woman becomes pregnant, the probability of complications increases.

The Metropolitan Life Insurance Company maintains that if a person is ten pounds overweight at the age of forty-five or above, his or her chances of premature death are 8 percent higher than the norm. With each additional pound the risk of premature death rises 1 percent.

People who are overfat will almost certainly live shorter lives, but that is not necessarily the worst of it. Their lives will be characterized by greater fatigue, restricted mobility, increased susceptibility to illness of every variety, and disqualification from a variety of fun and healthy activities. Keep in mind that these things are not caused by age, which is uncontrollable, but by excess weight which is controllable.

There's a good chance that you labor, as we once did, under the misconception that fat and excess weight are simply products of eating too much or too much of the wrong things. While what we eat is extremely important (as we'll see in the next chapter), dieting is not the only key to weight control.

I'll never forget when, six years ago, I determined to shed my excess fat (I was about thirty pounds overweight). I started running purely to lose weight, and I did, but in a few months I began to realize that according to the books my running was only burning off a few hundred calories a day. Yet my appetite had increased and though I was only eating good food, I was eating as much as four hundred calories per day more than before. So why was I losing weight?

Because regular aerobic exercise changes the metabolic rate of our bodies. The result is that we burn more calories not just when we exercise, but all day, even when we sleep. In other words, aerobic exercise doesn't just strengthen muscles and burn off a few hundred calories—it turns sluggish and inefficient fuel-burning bodies into the tuned-up and efficient fuel-burning machines they were intended to be.

Ever wondered why many overweight people eat less than skinny people, yet remain overweight? The reason is simply that their metabolism adjusts to their level of caloric intake. The less they eat, the slower their bodies burn calories. Consequently, they make no progress. Short of starving themselves to death, those slow-burning people (I'm one of them) will not lose weight apart from regular proper exercise, and even if they do they will almost certainly regain it. Diet alone cannot work because it fails to address the real problem—a sluggish metabolism in need of regular aerobic exercise. In short, such exercise is the ultimate and, for most, the only healthy cure for being overfat.

Furthermore, apparently non-fat or even skinny people may in fact have as much or more dangerous deposits of fat than outwardly fat people. They can be as physically unfit as their obviously fat counterparts.

We normally think of fat as located between the muscles and the skin. This is the fat that is visible to the eye, because it stretches the skin and makes it protrude. But fat also exists within the muscles themselves. It is marbled into the muscles to a lesser degree among the physically fit and to a greater degree among the unfit—regardless of their physical appearance.

Hence, people can be underweight and overfat. You may be envied by your friends because you have not gained a pound in the last ten years. But if you have not been exercising properly and regularly, and if you have been eating a typical American diet, you have probably gained ten pounds of fat while losing ten pounds of muscle. You may have no net weight gain, but your overall fitness is drastically worse. In fact, since muscle weighs more than fat, you may have even lost weight yet still be fatter than ever before in your life!

If it hasn't already, your metabolism will eventually change. For a while there may be no weight gain, but suddenly the fat that has already replaced your muscle will make its way to the outside of your muscles, and begin to accumulate between the muscle and the skin. You will then *see* the fat in the roll at your stomach, or the deposits on your arms, thighs, and bottom.

The average age for this metabolism change is thirty-five, but it may come much earlier or later. Once it happens, neither your fitness nor your weight can be effectively controlled by diet. By undereating, fat people will tend to look unhealthy—and be unhealthy—because they are losing more muscle than fat. They do not look much better because they lose weight in exactly the wrong places. Skinny people attempting to gain weight by eating without exercise will likewise gain weight in the wrong places, developing bulkier thighs, a puffy stomach, and a double chin.

Studies show it is not at all unusual for a non-exercising woman to have increased her body fat by 50 percent from age twenty to age thirty-five. Since women by nature have a higher percentage of fat than men (which increases their propensity toward fat), it is no surprise that obesity is a much more common problem among women than men.

The point of all this is not that fat is bad, simply that excess fat is bad. Body fat is essential. An acceptable fat range for men is 12-17 percent, for women 19-24 percent. Unfortunately, most men have as high a body fat percentage as women should, and most women are considerably higher still, averaging a very unhealthy 36 percent body fat.[1]

Curious about your percentage of body fat? There are a number of scientific methods to determine this, and many schools, health clubs, and hospitals have the necessary equipment. Call around in your area if you're interested.

Excess fat means excess physical stress—more strain on your heart, muscles and bones. It also means psychological stress—often overfat people don't feel good about themselves. Aerobic exercise will reduce excess fat . . . and, in the process, excess stress.

AEROBIC EXERCISE: WHAT WILL IT DO FOR YOU?

If aerobic exercise had no other benefits—even if it didn't take off an ounce of fat—what it does for the heart would more than justify it. The heart is the key to the functioning of the whole body. The healthier the heart the healthier the body. Like any muscle, the heart is strengthened through use. The more it is exercised the stronger, healthier, and more efficient and stress-resistant it becomes.

While major muscle groups are involved in any aerobic exercise, the muscle that does the most work is the heart. The increased oxygen demand of the muscles requires the heart to beat faster.

Those who exercise aerobically increase the size, strength, stamina, and efficiency of their hearts. Simply put, day in and day out their hearts do not have to work as hard to do their job, and they do their job better. Aerobic exercisers have far less chance of having a heart attack than an inactive person, and at least a four times greater chance of surviving one.

The difference between the heart of an aerobic exerciser and that of a non-exerciser of the same age is often remarkable. The blood flow can be as much as five times greater in the aerobic exerciser. This means good circulation, greater alertness, superior health, and greater ability to withstand stress.

But regular aerobic exercise does many other things for the body, some of which are listed below. If you do not do regular aerobic exercise, mark those benefits which you would particularly welcome. If you have been exercising aerobically for at least several months, mark those which you have already experienced, and note how many of these benefits are stress-related:

strengthens heart
strengthens muscles
improves muscle tone
improves digestion
improves waste elimination
improves muscle relaxation
improves circulation to extremities
improves quality of sleep
improves appearance
increases lung capacity
increases energy
increases stamina
increases healthy blood vessel growth
increases resistance to illness
increases coping ability

increases life span (barring accident or disease)
increases alertness
increases fuel burning efficiency
increases resistance to physical trauma
decreases recovery time
decreases harmful blood clotting
decreases blood fat and cholesterol levels
controls body fat and weight levels
releases tension
releases pent up emotions
decreases appetite
stabilizes blood sugar

THE PSYCHOLOGICAL BENEFITS OF EXERCISE

You may have been surprised to see on the list that aerobic exercise improves coping ability, releases tension, reduces pent-up emotions, decreases depression, and improves disposition. Do these claims seem exaggerated? They're not.

Remember the fight or flight syndrome? When confronted by a threat, our adrenaline skyrockets and we are mobilized to action. Unfortunately, since what threatens us is rarely physical, we are charged with physical tension but have no constructive way to release it.

This excess energy that otherwise works against us—turning into hypertension and ulcers—is released through aerobic exercise. It is a physical outlet or escape valve for physical tension.

Exercise improves our disposition in several ways. It makes us more lighthearted because it is a form of play. It takes us back to our childhood when we were active and playful. Play is a benign form of temporary escape from adult responsibilities and pressures. It is creative and recreative. Play fills up drained reservoirs and gives a sense of enjoyment and well-being that is hard to describe. If you've experienced it, you understand.

Some experts say that the rhythmic motion of such exercises as walking, running, bicycling, and swimming has a soothing effect that reduces anxiety.

But not all of this is psychological. Research has proven that aerobic exercise greatly increases the body's production of endorphins. These are natural pain killers. Perhaps you've experienced "runner's high." This condition is produced by endorphins.

Eight world class athletes were found to have an average endorphin level of 320 when at rest. After twelve minutes of aerobic exercise, their endorphins were at 1600—five times greater than normal. Fifteen minutes after stopping they were still at 1000, and thirty minutes later still over 400.

Endorphins are probably a major reason why aerobic exercise has been proven to counteract depression. In 1976, psychiatrist John Griest did a study at the University of Wisconsin that captured the amazing mental health potential of exercise. He put eight clinically depressed patients into a ten-week running program. The result? Six of the eight were cured of their depression. Griest admitted that this 75 percent cure rate was far higher than that achieved by psychotherapy or any other known counseling technique.[2]

If fitness decreases depression, lack of fitness increases it. It is therefore no surprise that women seeking professional help for depression are usually much less physically fit than the average woman.[3]

A friend who read the uncompleted manuscript of this chapter told us her daughter had been extremely moody for months, to the point that she felt she needed to take the girl out of school to give her more attention. She did this, but a few more months went by and she was still impossible to live with. With all else failing, this mother decided to bundle up (it was winter) and take her daughter for a walk every day. Within a week a dramatic change had taken place. The girl had received her mother's attention for months. But now she was getting daily exercise, and her disposition was transformed.

Skeptical? Let me tell you about Gail. She came to me for counseling five years ago. Severely and chronically depressed, Gail desperately reached out for help because she was not only contemplating suicide but was tempted to smother her own children in their sleep so they would not have to suffer the pain of their mother's death.

Gail needed more help than I could give her, so I linked her up with a professional counselor. Things stabilized somewhat, but even with the counseling Gail was far from out of the woods.

When I saw Gail two months later, I was shocked. She looked sharp, perky, and happy. She'd lost weight, but the incredible change was in her countenance. She was radiant—completely transformed.

"What happened?" I asked.

"You wouldn't believe it," she said. "Seven weeks ago I started an aerobics class and since then I've been a different woman. The terrible thoughts that plagued me for so long are gone. My mind has cleared and I'm feeling great."

Perhaps Gail's exercise corrected a chemical imbalance. Perhaps feeling better physically helped her turn the corner to feeling better mentally. Maybe looking better physically allowed her to break through her poor self-image. Perhaps it was meeting other Christian women in the aerobics class, or maybe it was the endorphins induced by exercise. Whatever the reason, the bottom line is that exercise gave Gail a new lease on life. It may actually have saved her life.

(We hasten to add that many psychological problems will *not* disappear with exercise. Our point is simply that exercise *may* have substantial psychological benefits.)

HOW TO EXERCISE AEROBICALLY

Let's get into the specifics of this wonderful exercise that can do so much for our bodies, minds, and emotions.

Aerobic exercise works the body's muscles hard enough to increase their demand for oxygen but not hard enough to run them out of oxygen. An exercise must be two things to qualify as aerobic:

It must be steady and continuous for at least 15 minutes, preferably 20-30.

It must raise the heartbeat to 70-85 percent of its maximum capacity and keep it in that range throughout the duration of the exercise.

In order to follow the second guideline, you need to determine your ideal pulse target range when exercising. Subtract your age from 226 to get your maximum heart rate (men should subtract from 220). Multiply this number by .70 to get your minimum target rate and .85 to get your maximum target rate.

For instance, if you're thirty-three years old, your maximum heart rate is about 193. Your minimum aerobic target rate is 135, your maximum is 164. Your ideal would be to stay as close to the middle (150) as possible throughout the duration of your exercise. If you're fifty-five your maximum rate is 171, your target range 120-145. (This will work *unless* you have an unusually slow or fast pulse. If slow—65 or less—stay near the bottom of your target range. If fast—95 or more—stay near the top.)

Now that you know your target range, you must know how to take your exercise pulse. It's done the same way as taking your resting pulse, by pressing the fingers against the wrist, temple, or neck. But instead of counting for sixty seconds you must only count for six seconds, because you will normally have to stop exercising to do it. When you do, your pulse will begin to slow immediately, making a longer count invalid, as well as interrupting what needs to be continuous exercise.

After taking your pulse for six seconds, simply multiply the count by ten. Your goal is to always keep your pulse within your heart rate target zone. If it is too high, slow down. If it is too low, speed up. If you keep your pulse in its target range for at least 15-20 minutes, you have done a full-fledged aerobic exercise and have taken your first step to a longer and better life.

The beauty of aerobic exercise is that it molds itself perfectly to each person. By walking briskly enough to keep her heart beat in the target range, a fifty-year-old woman who may be twenty pounds overweight is getting just as good exercise as the twenty-one-year-old college athlete who zooms by her. Their speeds may differ radically, but the benefits to their hearts, lungs and metabolisms are equal.

As you become more fit you will need to increase your speed to keep your heart rate up. But this is no problem—it won't feel any harder to you, because you'll be in better condition. As your condition improves you will naturally walk faster, run faster, bike faster, or swim faster with no more effort. Just don't go under or over your target range.

WHICH EXERCISES ARE AEROBIC?

Not all forms of exercise are aerobic—in fact, most aren't. Housework may be hard work, but it is not aerobic. Why? Because its intensity rarely if ever lifts your heart rate to its target range, and even if it does it doesn't keep it there anywhere close to 15-20 minutes in succession. You can play tennis for two hours, and you'll exercise a lot of muscles and burn some calories, but when you pause between points or have a steady rally without much movement, your pulse plunges below the minimum target rate. Any sport or activity with breaks or significant slow-downs between bursts of energy is not aerobic.

So which exercises are aerobic? Here are some of them:

Outdoor Aerobic Exercises	*Indoor Aerobic Exercises*
running or jogging	stationary bicycle
brisk walking	rowing machine
bicycling	jumping rope
swimming	trampoline
cross-country skiing	treadmill
	swimming
	continuous calisthenics or dancing

Fine books have been written that explain the ins and outs of these exercises. We particularly recommend Covert Bailey's *Fit or Fat?*, which is one of the simplest and best explanations of aerobic exercise we've read.[4]

QUESTIONS ABOUT AEROBIC EXERCISE

Have some questions about aerobic exercise? Here are some of the most common ones:

177

1. Should I exercise alone or with someone? If you need accountability, exercise with a friend. It's much harder to rationalize skipping your exercise if someone else is counting on you. It's also great fun and fellowship. Furthermore, a key test of aerobic exercise is that you are slightly winded but not so much that you can't talk. Carrying on a conversation while walking, biking, or jogging is therefore a good test.

Another major benefit to exercising with someone else is that it makes time fly. I usually run alone, but when I'm running with someone else I'm always amazed at how quickly the time passes. One more plus—exercising with someone else is always safer. You don't want to be alone and two miles from home with an accident, injury, or someone—whether with two feet or four—harassing you (this is rare in most places though).

2. When should I exercise? Whatever time of day is best for you. Early morning before your responsibilities start, mid-morning after the kids are in school, early afternoon, late afternoon (as a pick-me-up and appetite depressant before dinner), or early evening. Late evening is usually not best because it is hard to get to sleep within an hour or two of exercise.

For most people it's best to exercise at least an hour after eating. Why? To avoid cramps and because blood goes to your stomach to aid digestion, and you need blood in your extremities during aeorbic exercise.

3. Where should I exercise? For an outdoor exercise, find a favorite place or route close to home. For walking and biking, seek out hills. If you run, beware of traffic. Air pollution fights against the lung benefits of exercise, not to mention the aesthetics of the whole thing (one study says that daily running in polluted inner cities is equivalent to smoking two packs of cigarettes a day).

4. How often should I exercise? Three days a week is minimal, four or five preferable. Most people can handle six, but everyone should have a weekly day off for recuperation.

If you exercise three to four days a week, make it every other day—don't go two days in a row then take two off. Twenty-five minutes four days a week is much better than fifty minutes two days a week. A good schedule for many people is three days on, one off. Unless you are injured or ill, don't take off two or three days in a row, or you'll start losing your hard-gained benefits.

5. How do I get started? Crash exercise programs are as unnatural, potentially harmful, and self-defeating as crash diets. Start slowly. In your eagerness to get going don't push it. It may have taken you twenty years to get out of shape. It will take you at least several months to start getting back in shape.

If you have been inactive a long time, start with only 10-15 minutes every other day. Try just walking first, then something more strenuous as you build up endurance. You may not be able to do a full-fledged aerobic exercise at first, but you'll work up to it within a few weeks.

6. Should I consult my doctor before starting? If you've been very inactive, are pregnant, are over sixty or have medical problems—especially heart disease, by all means talk with your doctor before you start exercising. He or she will almost certainly encourage you to exercise, but check to be sure. Your doctor may have some guidelines and cautions for you and advise you as to which exercise would be best in your situation (it's likely that he'll recommend exercise-walking). If you're pregnant and you've been exercising for some time, you'll probably be able to continue, but your doctor may advise you against beginning an aerobics program during pregnancy.

If you suffer from excess dizziness, nausea, heart palpitations or other adverse symptoms stop exercising and consult your physician.

MISCELLANEOUS GUIDELINES FOR AEROBIC EXERCISE

Don't exercise through pain. "No pain, no gain" is for macho women, not you.

Drink liquids before and after exercise. Your body needs extra liquids whether or not you're thirsty.

Avoid exercising in hot temperatures. If you exercise outdoors in warm weather, do it in the morning or evening.

Wear proper clothing. In cold weather wear several thin layers instead of one thick one. Cover your head and you'll be amazed how warm exercising will get you. In warm weather, dress light. Never wear rubberized or airtight suits—they don't allow your body the air and circulation essential during exercise.

Always warm up before you exercise. Stretching is the best way to do this. Stretching is important to everyone, but the older you are the more important it is. It increases your flexibility and decreases the adverse effects on your joints, ligaments, and muscles. Many injuries could be prevented by proper stretching prior to exercise.

After stretching, begin a slow version of your exercise. If you are going to walk, walk slowly, if you're going to run, run slowly. Bike slowly or swim slowly at the beginning, then after two to three minutes start picking it up. By five minutes you can be at your normal pace. However, be sure you don't start counting your exercise as aerobic until you are at your normal pace.

End your exercise by reversing this process. Slow down gradually rather than stopping abruptly. Never end your exercise with a sprint. Then, when you finally do stop, stretch again. Studies show that post-exercise stretching is almost as important as pre-exercise stretching.

If you choose to do other exercises, perhaps such floor exercises as sit-ups and leg-lifts, do them after aerobics rather than before. They are better done when your body is warmed up anyway, and you don't want to rob energy from your aerobics by doing them first.

POPULAR REASONS FOR NOT EXERCISING

With all it has to offer us, aerobic exercise should not be a phase or a fad to toy with for a few weeks or months. It should be a lifestyle. If we are not bedridden, ill, or injured, aerobic exercise should be as much a part of our lives as eating and sleeping. The popular reasons for not exercising deserve a closer look.

"I don't have enough time." Exercising five days per week,

thirty minutes per day uses 1.5 percent of your week, and it may add years to your life. If you don't take enough time now, you may have less time to live later!

"I don't have enough energy." Experts maintain that every forty-five minutes of exercise produces approximately one extra hour of usable energy.[5] In the long run, exercise gives more energy than it takes. If you need more energy you probably need more exercise.

Nanci says that without fail it's the days when she invests the time and energy to do her aerobics that she has more energy to clean the house and perform her other duties. She can do more in five hours when she has exercised than eight hours when she hasn't.

"I don't have enough money." How much does it cost to walk or run?

"Exercise is boring." Even if it was boring, exercise would still be worth doing, but it doesn't have to be boring. If you walk, run, or bicycle, change the scenery. Find new places. Exercise with a friend or two. Join a class.

If you are rowing, jumping rope, using a mini-trampoline or a stationary bicycle, you can still listen to music or even talk to someone. You could call up a friend who is stationary bicycling at the same time and talk to her for thirty minutes. You may both huff and puff a bit, but you still should be able to talk. Meanwhile you're holding each other accountable to exercise.

"I'm embarrassed to exercise in public." So don't. Choose one of the many aerobic exercises you can do in your home.

Keep in mind though that few people make fun of someone who is exercising. Usually they will respect you for trying to get in shape rather than ridicule you for the shape you're in.

"I just don't have the self-discipline to exercise daily." Don't sell yourself short. In some areas you probably have lots of discipline. Do you get up in the morning, fix meals, go to work, wash the dishes, and clean house even when you don't feel like it? Then you're practicing self-discipline. You can do it with exercise too.

How Exercising Right Relieves Stress

Try a system of positive reinforcement. After each exercise, reward yourself with some juice and popcorn, a thirty minute break, a favorite magazine—anything that adds more motivation and fun to exercising. I save up things I really want to read, then don't let myself read them until I'm on my exercise bike. Often I stay on the bike longer just to finish a chapter or article.

WHAT ARE YOU WAITING FOR?

I ran in a 10K (6.2 miles) race in which I watched a trim silver-haired lady, probably in her sixties, who was in great shape. I got a real good look at her . . . when she breezed by me on the fourth mile. Nothing is so beautiful or inspiring as a vibrant, cheerful older woman who has exercised to get in top shape.

If you begin and stick with a program of aerobic exercise four or five times a week, you will probably start to see and feel a difference in four weeks—particularly if you follow the nutritional guidelines set forth in the following chapter. In eight weeks the difference may be substantial. But some people do not show such immediate progress. Allow yourself four months to really evaluate the results—physically, mentally, emotionally, even spiritually. If you keep it up for six or eight months you won't believe the difference, and you'll never again be content with the sedentary life.

Do you want to be healthier? Do you want to be happier? Do you want to have fun and be fun? Do you want to live long enough and have enough energy to swing your grandchildren in the park? Then exercise aerobically. For life.

FOOD FOR THOUGHT AND DISCUSSION

1. Many people believe that body fat can be lost by dieting alone. What's the problem with this approach?

2. Why is it that some overweight people eat much less than slender people yet remain overweight?

3. "You can be overfat without being overweight. agree or disagree? Explain.

4. What are some common reasons for not exercising. your response to each?

5. What aerobic exercises have you tried? Which have you liked the best, and why?

6. If you have exercised aerobically over a period of at least a few months, what are some of the benefits you've seen as a result?

7. Can exercise or lack of exercise relate in any way to your spiritual life? Explain.

8. "The best reason I can think of for establishing and maintaining a regular program of aerobic exercise is_____
_____ ."

1. Covert Bailey, *Fit or Fat* (Boston: Houghton Mifflin Co., 1977), p. 8.
2. Keith W. Sehnert, *Stress/Unstress* (Minneapolis: Augsburg Publishing House, 1981), p. 173.
3. Marilyn Elias, "Depressed? Running Will Help," *USA Today*, 2 April 1984, p. 2D.
4. Covert Bailey, *Fit or Fat* (Houghton Mifflin Co., 1977).
5. Christine Ann Leatz, *Unwinding* (Englewood Cliffs, N.J.: Prentice-Hall, 1981), p. 121.

11

HOW EATING RIGHT
REDUCES STRESS

Research indicates that at least a third of our stress is caused by what we eat.[1] Even the stress caused by other sources is compounded by our diet. Good nutritional habits, however, increase our ability to face life's demands.

Meet Fran, who's a fashion designer. She begins her day by dragging herself out of bed and rushing off to the office. If she has an extra ten minutes she stops for breakfast (using the term loosely) at the fast food place (the sign on the door says "exceeded," but the question is "exceeded what?"). She usually gets pancakes made from refined flour with added sugar soaked in high-fat butter or margarine and immersed with sugar-filled syrup. Or maybe she's nutrition-conscious (so she thinks), so she has a fat-ridden sausage between two pieces of muffin made with bleached flour and sugar. Of course she has two or three cups of coffee to wash it down.

Fran then proceeds to the office where she will take a 10:30 coffee and donut break, then go back to her desk till lunch. Her lunch consists of white bread, red meat, deep fried potatoes, and a cola. After a sluggish afternoon, Fran drags herself home to a quick-dinner-in-a-can entree and an evening spent snacking on chips and pop, and maybe a dish of ice cream (dairy products are one of the four essential food groups, right?).

Meanwhile, Fran's sister's nutritional day began when she downed the two half waffles left by her husband and kids. *How can they stand so much syrup?* she wonders. For lunch Janice has a wholesome bowl of soup and a small salad. But, of course she can't waste Johnny's unfinished peanut butter and jelly sandwich, so down it goes and if there's no backwash in his glass of milk, it goes too.

In the animal world, those who eat what others leave behind are called scavengers. In our world, they are called mothers.

By the afternoon Janice is exhausted but has to start dinner. *Why not just whip together some Hamburger Helper?* she thinks. *The family loves it, especially if there's apple pie for dessert* (what could be better for you than apples?).

After the kids are in bed, Janice plops down by her husband

in her matching recliner. She wonders where her energy has gone and concludes that she is just getting old.

Janice's eating habits remain the same, and so does her run-down condition. But six months ago Fran determined to get serious about nutrition. The difference has been remarkable. Fran is more energetic, less fatigued, and generally more fun to be with. She has a new bounce in her step and even finds herself getting along better with her boss. Fran looks and feels better, and feels better about herself.

THE TRUTH ABOUT SUGAR

Glucose, a form of sugar, is essential to the brain and the entire body. However, the body converts most food into glucose in a steady and systematic way while providing the proper nutrients it needs. In other words, even if we never ate table sugar (sucrose), our body would produce from good foods all the sugar we need.

When a large quantity of sucrose is ingested into the body, there is a dramatic physical reaction which throws out of balance the normal process of glucose production. Sugar was meant to be consumed in small quantities as it naturally appears in foods.

The pancreas routinely produces insulin in order to properly deal with the glucose the body produces. But, in a thirty minute period, a piece of apple pie and a scoop of ice cream requires insulin production to increase by one hundred times.[2] This places extreme and immediate demands on the pancreas to produce insulin in order to "put out the fire" caused by the sugar. This can raise our heart beat and our blood pressure and lead to hypoglycemic (low blood sugar) reactions and eventual obesity, with all its health hazards.

Close your eyes and envision twenty-five 5-pound bags of sugar. If you are the average American, you eat this much sugar every year. If you weigh 125 pounds, this means you consume your own weight in sugar annually! A full 25 percent of our total calorie intake comes from the two-and-a-half pounds of sugar we average per week. That two-and-a-half pounds per

187

week, by the way, is precisely the amount of sugar our great great grandparents ate per year.[3]

Sugar that is added to foods contains only empty calories, meaning that it normally has no nutritional value, nothing positive to offer the body. By taking the place of real food, sugar robs the body of the nutrients it should and probably would have received if the sugar hadn't been eaten.

Sugar is a mood drug. Much hypertension, headaches, irritability, impatience, and general edginess, as well as hyperactivity and sleeplessness in children and adults, has been linked to excess sugar consumption. We're convinced that the high stress levels of the holidays—which are normally attributed to other factors—are also significantly influenced by the greatly increased intake of sugar.

HIDDEN SUGAR

You might be saying, "Well, there's no way I eat that much sugar. We don't even have a sugar bowl in the house!"

You don't have to have a sugar bowl. Sugar is laced through many of the foods you eat every day.

Fruits, already high in natural sugar (fructose), are canned in heavy, sugary syrup. Bottled salad dressing, canned meats and vegetables, frozen dinners and most other convenience foods contain sugar. How pervasive is sugar in our food? Even *salt* contains sugar!

Most dry cereals range from 10 to 58 percent sugar.[4] If you turn to "natural" granola cereals you're usually still getting one or two added teaspoons of sugar per serving. Shredded Wheat, Puffed Rice (and Wheat), Nutri-Grain Wheat (and Corn), and Grape Nuts are some of the very few cereals without sugar.

A one-ounce Hershey's Chocolate bar, a Snickers, a Nestle's Crunch, and a Nature Valley Granola Cluster all contain about 3 1/2 teaspoons of sugar.

Soda pops usually contain eight to eleven teaspoons of sugar, as do twelve-ounce servings of Tang, Hi-C, and Kool-

Aid. In order to really visualize this, add ten teaspoons of sugar in a glass. It's amazing how much sugar we consume without even thinking. Here are some popular commercial food products and their percentages of refined sugar:

Jello Cherry Gelatin Dessert	82.6%
Coffee-Mate Non-Dairy Creamer	65.4%
Cremora Non-Dairy Creamer	56.9%
Hershey's Milk Chocolate	51.4%
Shake 'N Bake Barbeque Style	50.9%
Sara Lee Chocolate Original Butter Recipe Cake	35.9%
Wish Bone Russian Dressing	30.2%
Heinz Tomato Ketchup	28.9%
Quaker 100% Natural Cereal	23.9%
Hamburger Helper	23.0%
Sealtest Chocolate Ice Cream	21.4%
Birds Eye Cool Whip	21.0%
Libby's Sliced Peaches	17.9%
Wyler's Beef Boullion Cubes	14.8%
Dannon Blueberry Low Fat Yogurt	13.7%
Ritz Crackers	11.8%
Del Monte Whole Kernel Corn	10.7%
Skippy Creamy Peanut Butter	9.2%
Ragu Spaghetti Sauce	6.2%

WHAT CAN I DO TO CUT BACK ON SUGAR?

Take a closer look at food labels. By law, ingredients must be listed in order of their prominence. Is sugar one of the first?

Often, however, it's not that simple. Despite the fact that there are many other kinds of sugar, sucrose or table sugar is the only one which the FDA requires to be called sugar. So, if you see any of the following on a label, translate it "sugar": sucrose, glucose, fructose, lactose, maltose, dextrose, sorbitol, manitol, and disaccharide. If you feel any relief when you read corn syrup, honey, or molasses, don't. They are forms of sugar, and they have normally been added to the food rather than appearing naturally in it.

Beware—products can say "artificially sweetened" and still contain sugar. You can only be sure they're sugarless if they say "sugarless" or "sugar free."

Consider using sugar substitutes. The artificial sweetener debate goes on, and there are still concerns about both saccharin and aspartame (Nutra Sweet is the primary brand). Many doctors recommend aspartame, as long as it is consumed in small quantities, preferably in only a few items per day.

Rediscover nature's desserts: fruits. Prior to the production of refined sugar, sweet tooths were satisfied by fruits. While fructose is a form of sugar, when eaten with the pulp and fiber of its fruit it does not have the dramatic effect on the body that it does when isolated from its fruit. Plus, it is more filling and satisfying.

Thanks to our obsession with sugar, our tastes have been dulled to the natural sweetness of fruits. But your taste buds can be retrained so you can actually take more delight in a strawberry than a piece of candy.

CIVILIZED DISEASES

Refined sugar is only one feature of our nutritional wasteland. Refined or white flour is equally stripped of its fiber and nutrients, and equally pervasive. It is the primary ingredient in bread, biscuits, muffins, pancake mixes, crackers, pasta, noodles, baking mixes of all varieties, cakes, cookies, pastries and pie crusts (often refined flour and sugar are combined).

British physician Dennis P. Burkitt spent twenty years studying cancer and other diseases common to industrialized countries—especially cancer of the colon, cancer of the rectum, diverticulitus, colitis, diabetes, and coronary heart disease. He also researched less serious but very common disorders such as gall stones, hemorrhoids, constipation, and various intestinal problems. All these diseases and disorders are often related to stress.

Dr. Burkitt found that these diseases were virtually nonexistent among African tribes. Until, that is, these tribes became westernized in lifestyle and began eating the same refined foods that we eat.[5]

Their diets had been high in grains, fruits, and vegetables, and low in meat and fat. Once westernized, they ate far less fiber, far more fat, and for the first time they ate refined sugar and flour. In a short period all of the debilitating diseases mentioned above began to appear in these tribes.

Those tribes not yet westernized consume 50-150 grams of fiber per day—while American and western Europeans average only 25 grams per day.

WHAT FIBER DOES

Obviously, then, fiber is an important ingredient for any diet. But what exactly is fiber? It is the indigestible portion of whole grains, nuts, seeds, beans, vegetables, and fruits (including their skins and seeds).

Fiber absorbs water, softens the stool, and loosens bowel movements, thereby helping to prevent diverticulitis and hemorrhoids. By decreasing the amount of time food spends in the body, fiber apparently lowers the caloric absorption rate and lowers the incidence of disease that is created by the decomposition of waste products that remain too long in the digestive tract. Hence, fiber is a major deterrent to colon cancer and related diseases.

Fiber also improves glucose tolerance and lowers cholesterol. Because it is bulky, it fills you up faster and requires that you chew it thoroughly, making the meal last longer. Consequently your stomach sends the "full" message to your brain before you overeat. As a result—and since fiber itself contains no calories—many people lose weight when they do nothing else but significantly increase their fiber intake.

HOW DO I GET MORE FIBER INTO MY DIET?

Buy, bake with, and use mixes high in whole grains—wheat, oats, rye, barley or corn.

Serve brown rice instead of white, whole wheat breads and pasta instead of refined or white breads and pasta.

Eat high-fiber cereals, especially whole wheat. But be careful—most high-fiber cereals contain sugar, and those that don't may be high in salt.

Add fiber to foods. Add wheat germ, wheat bran, oat bran, bran cereal or oatmeal to foods like meatloaves and chilis. Or you may substitute them for part of your regular ingredients in breads, muffins and rolls.

Add cooked, dried beans to soups and stews. Add beans and nuts to salads (try spoon-sized shredded wheat for croutons). When recipes call for chocolate chips, use nuts, raisins, chopped figs, dates, or prunes.

Eat high-fiber snacks such as popcorn—preferably without butter or salt. Stay away from low-fiber and high-fat snacks such as potato chips, pretzels, and highly processed crackers.

Eat more high-fiber raw fruits—apples, pears, raisins, prunes, and blackberries.

When possible, eat fruits and vegetables with the skin on. They are high both in fiber and nutrition. When the seeds are small, eat them too.

CARBOHYDRATES, PROTEINS, AND FATS

Notice that the high-fiber foods are carbohydrates. Because sugar is a carbohydrate, many people mistakenly believe carbos are the dieter's enemy, but sugar is a *simple* carbohydrate. Vegetables, grains, and seeds are *complex* carbohydrates. These carbos break down more slowly and are essential to physical health.

The irony is that while sugar consumption has skyrocketed, consumption of complex carbohydrates has plummeted.

One of the finest popular diets is the Pritikin Diet.[6] It is low in refined sugar, fat and cholesterol, low to moderate in protein, and very high in complex carbohydrates. It is not a temporary weight-loss diet, but a long-term lifestyle diet you can stick with.

Some diets and health regimens push protein above all else. Protein is certainly essential, but unfortunately we often try to get it from the worst sources—red meats.

We need 50-100 calories of fat per day. But most of us consume ten times that, some many more (a Big Mac and regular fries alone contains 400 calories of fat). In 1900, 30 percent of the average American diet was fat. Today it is 45 percent fat. Combine that with our calories from sugar and you have a diet that is 75 percent fat and sugar, both of which, in excess, become body fat. This is an alarming level.

Popular foods such as beef, ham, bacon, and luncheon meats are high in saturated fats and cholesterol, and when eaten regularly over the long haul they are detrimental to the heart. (Perhaps one of the reasons God forbade Israel from eating pork was that it was so high in fat and filled with harmful parasites—laboratory tests demonstrate that many of these parasites can live for hours even in a 500 degree oven).

If you do eat red meats you must realize you are eating large portions of fat and cholesterol. Eighty percent of the total calories in prime rib are fat, not protein. When you trim off the fat from the steak, you've only eliminated a portion of it. The rest of the fat—the majority of it—is marbled throughout the steak. Likewise, 72 percent of the calories in a typical hamburger are fat, 79 percent in bacon, 80 percent in wieners, and 84 percent in pork sausage.

WHAT CAN I DO TO EAT LESS FAT?

Instead of red meats such as beef and pork, eat fish and chicken turkey and other fowl. These make great sandwiches, and many people find they prefer a chicken enchilada to a beef enchilada

Eat vegetables, especially split peas, dried beans and lentils. These are the best sources of protein. Peanut butter is a high protein source without cholesterol (which comes only from animals), but it is still very high in fat. Vegetarian sandwiches on whole wheat bread can be delicious—it's amazing how little you miss the meat!

Avoid meat gravy, lard, and shortening. If you must use a butter-type spread, use margarine (preferably from a tub) or one

193

of the light spreads (but realize they are still high in fat and should only be eaten in moderation).

Avoid deep-fried foods. They are extremely high in saturated fat. Not only is the high fat bad for you, but the calorie increase is phenomenal. One cup of a boiled or baked potato contains 118 calories. When cut and french-fried, the same potato contains 456 calories!

If you must use cooking oil, use polyunsaturated oils such as vegetable, corn, peanut and safflower oils. Realize, though, that while such oils may appear to be natural, in the strictest sense they're not. They have been stripped of their natural husk and fiber, and one ingredient (fat) has been unnaturally extracted for use in megadose quantities. (Did you know that it takes several hundred ears of corn to make a single cup of corn oil?)

Choose your salad dressings carefully. Many of them—such as a typical thousand island and even some of the "low cal" dressings—are laden with fat. Learn to enjoy a good salad without burying it in fat.

If you drink milk, be sure it's non-fat (skim) or low-fat (1 or 2 percent). Whole milk and milk products are a primary source of excess fat. When possible, use low-fat cheese, low-fat cottage cheese, and low-fat yogurt (careful—most yogurt is high in sugar).

Because fats are difficult for the body to digest, when you cut back on them you and your family may experience fewer stomach and bowel regularity problems.

JUNK FOOD

Junk food is almost well-named. Junk it is. But food it isn't. People who wouldn't dream of pouring mud and water into their car's gas tank do worse things to their own body. It is ironic that our society worships thinness and then uses thin actresses to promote the consumption of the very things that make people fat.

An eight-ounce bag of potato chips contains an incredible 1200 calories and 80 grams of fat, and puffed cheese snacks contain even more. You may not be overweight, but these products will make you grossly overfat. Some resign themselves to munching on crackers, but many crackers are high in fat, sugar and sodium. Read the labels before you buy.

It requires a degree in chemistry to read the list of ingredients in most junk food. It's full of preservatives and flavor enhancers with names like propyl gallate, monosodium glutamate, and sodium tripolyphosphate (sound nutritious?). The rule of thumb is, the shorter the list and the shorter the names of the ingredients, the better. We hate to make a habit of eating things we can't even pronounce.

While it's important for everyone to avoid too many chemical additives, it's particularly critical for pregnant women. (They should also watch carefully what medications they take, and should cut out or way down on artificial sweeteners, colas, and coffee.)

SALT

Excess salt (sodium chloride) is a leading contributor to hypertension, which in turn leads to strokes and heart attacks, the nation's leading killers. Too much salt is hard on the kidneys, and can cause edginess and irritability, as well as raising blood pressure. It is a major cause of stress.

High blood pressure is very rare in populations with low sodium intakes. Since sixty million Americans suffer from high blood pressure already, it is imperative that we cut our salt intake to a minimum.

Though sodium is essential to the body, it is almost impossible not to get enough of it from the foods we normally eat. The average American eats 5000 milligrams of sodium per day—more than twenty times what he needs.[7] Unfortunately, like sugar, salt is laced throughout many foods, serving as both preservative and flavoring. Most rice cereals are high in salt, as are processed meats, sauces, canned vegetables, and tomato and vegetable juices. And, of course, most chips, nuts and other prepared snacks are full of salt (high fat and high sodium often go together).

HOW DO I OVERCOME THE SALT HABIT?

Cut back your salt intake even if at first food tastes bland. Salt-craving is an acquired and self-perpetuating taste. The less salt you're used to eating the more naturally salty things taste. The more salt you eat, the blander food without salt tastes, and the more you think you need it. Cut back your intake, and your taste buds will eventually become more sensitive to food.

Learn which foods are high in salt. You can't cut down on salt without knowing where the salt really is. Sometimes this is surprising. Take typical fast foods like a cheeseburger, french fries, milkshake, and apple pie. Which of these contains the most salt? Most people think the fries do. Wrong. The fries have plenty of salt, but they contain the least. The milkshake has twice as much salt as the fries, the apple pie four times as much, and the cheeseburger over seven times as much!

Cut out the high fat and high sugar foods and you'll cut out lots of salt too.

Try using herbs and spices to season your foods.

Never salt before you taste, seldom salt after you taste, remove the salt shaker from the table, and use less salt in cooking. Salt draws out vitamins from foods under heat. But even without salt, water dissolves the nutrients in foods and heat often destroys them. Many canned or frozen vegetables, when boiled in water, lose most of their nutritional value. The water you throw away may contain more nutrients than the vegetables you eat. So, eat more fresh raw vegetables, and when you need to cook them, microwave them without water or steam them (food steamers are good, inexpensive investments).

Gradually cut back on salt in your cooking and your family probably won't even notice. Start your children out right by giving them unsalted baby food. Many baby foods are full of salt, because mothers often taste the food to decide if their baby will like it. Since adults are so used to salt, most won't like—and therefore won't buy—unsalted baby food. Let's be careful not to hook our children on something that later could threaten their health.

CAFFEINE

Caffeine is a drug which increases the heart rate, restricts blood vessels, and raises blood pressure. It stimulates the production of the primary stress hormone, adrenaline. Just two cups of coffee as much as triples the amount of adrenaline in the body.

Caffeine has a half-life of four to ten hours, meaning it affects you long after you want it to. It inhibits relaxation, causes sleeplessness, and decreases the quality of sleep. It puts people on edge and leaves them more irritable. In some cases it has been linked to bladder cancer. Furthermore, caffeine may stimulate the appetite and thereby promote overeating, and in some cases obesity.

Caffeine in all of its sources (not just coffee) has been found to contribute to fibrocystic disease, a sometimes pre-cancerous disease characterized by tender lumps and general sensitivity in the breasts. Many women have almost eliminated this disease simply by eliminating caffeine from their diet.

Both Nanci and I love a good cup of coffee. But we've cut way back over the years because caffeinated coffee is a stress-producer and we don't need more stress. Nanci quit drinking caffeinated coffee four years ago. After an awful week of withdrawal, she noticed a marked increase in her patience, tolerance level, and overall sense of well-being. Coffee is at its worst when taken in large quantities (three cups or more), and on an empty stomach.

If you argue that that a cup of coffee makes you feel better, you are simply acknowledging your caffeine addiction. We Christians who wouldn't dream of popping "uppers" drink coffee all day without blinking. Yet most stay-alert drugs contain 100 milligrams of caffeine—the same as a single small cup of coffee.[8] Drinking three cups is like taking a triple dose. In fact, four small cups or two to three mugs of coffee pump over five hundred milligrams of caffeine into your body. This amount of caffeine is particularly potent when taken on an empty stomach.

197

Many non-coffee drinkers are also caffeine addicts. You may prefer tea because of its taste or because it's easier on your stomach, but most teas contain around 75 percent as much caffeine as coffee. Many herbal teas contain no or little caffeine, but you should check to find out for sure.

An average twelve-ounce cola contains almost half as much caffeine as a cup of coffee. And caffeine can't be avoided just by staying off colas. According to FDA information, the top seven soft drinks in order of highest caffeine content are Diet Mr. Pibb (over 50 milligrams), Mountain Dew, Tab, Sunkist Orange, Shasta Cola, Dr. Pepper, and Sugar Free Dr. Pepper. They are followed closely by Pepsi, RC, and Coke (34 milligrams). The combination of 8-11 teaspoons of sugar and 40 milligrams of caffeine per can makes the regular consumption of soft drinks a potential health hazard.

Chocolate contains a caffeine-like substance which affects the body almost identically to caffeine. Some have linked it to hyperactivity, irritability, and learning problems in children. When you consider the amount of caffeine many children consume in soda pops and chocolate candy and ice cream, this is a major problem. Keep in mind too that because their bodies are smaller, the same amount of caffeine will have much greater effect on them than on an adult.

Caffeine is also prominent in pain-relievers. It is especially high in Cope, Anacin, and Vanquish, and extremely high in Excedrin. In fact, if you take the maximum daily dosage of Excedrin, you are taking the caffeine equivalent of six cups of coffee or twelve cans of cola! This is particularly ironic since you need to rest when you are sick, yet these caffeine laden pain-relievers raise your heart rate and blood pressure.

Now consider the combined effects of all these caffeine sources. It isn't uncommon for a woman in a single day to take several pain-relievers, down a few cups of coffee or tea and a soda or two (remember, diet sodas are just as high in caffeine) and maybe a chocolate dessert. The cumulative result is much more caffeine—and much more stress—than the body is designed to cope with.

WANT TO BREAK THE CAFFEINE HABIT?

Get off caffeine slowly. Sudden withdrawal may upset your balance, giving you headaches and leaving you tired and irritable.

Switch to decaffeinated coffee, tea, and soda pop, or to fruit juices, mineral water, or ice water. If you need something warm, try warm milk, cereal beverages (such as Postum) or plain heated water. Many people find that it really wasn't the taste of coffee or tea they enjoyed as much as just consuming a warm liquid.

Eat good nutritious meals. Addictions to caffeine, nicotine, and sugar all reinforce each other, and often relate to the fact that your body is craving good food. You may be eating enough, but if you're not eating the right foods your cravings will intensify.

Substitute exercise for coffee breaks. A short, brisk walk with deep breathing provides a healthy pick-me-up with no negative aftereffects. (Remember how recess rejuvenated you as a school child?)

In short, it may taste good to the last drop, but it isn't good for you. Times like these were made to break the caffeine habit. Fill it to the rim . . . with fruit juice.

THE GREAT VITAMIN CONTROVERSY

Everyone agrees that a variety of vitamins and minerals is essential to our health. Not everyone agrees, however, where those vitamins and minerals can and should come from. Many doctors and dieticians believe that a balanced diet supplies all the nutrients we need, and vitamin supplements are at best superfluous, and at worst potentially harmful.[9]

It is certainly true that the best way to get our vitamins is from food, where they occur naturally and are best assimilated into the body. Supplements are not a cure-all to compensate for poor eating habits. However, some people can receive benefits from vitamin supplements. Women in their childbearing years often need to take iron to replace what is lost during their menstrual periods. Insufficient iron is a common cause of stress and fatigue among women. Women who are pregnant or breast-feeding usually need more iron, folic acid, calcium, and vitamin A. The elderly, inactive, and those suffering from particular diseases may likewise need specific vitamin and mineral supplements, and should ask the advice of their doctor or dietician.

Vitamin megadoses are another matter. While megadoses mean megabucks for vitamin companies, many medical experts are skeptical and fearful of them. For most of us, one multiple vitamin with minerals each day should be more than sufficient. While most of the vitamins will not be absorbed by the body, hopefully if there is any shortage the body will benefit. To many, this prospect is worth the cost of the vitamins.

GUIDELINES FOR EATING RIGHT

Eat a good breakfast. Eat light at night—the later the lighter. If you must eat late at night, eat a small amount of complex carbohydrates, such as whole-grain bread, cereal, vegetables, or popcorn.

Try to keep a regular eating schedule that's right for you. Waiting too long between meals may cause you stress, in the form of headaches, nervousness, irritability, and loss of concentration and efficiency. An orange or apple may be just what you need to carry you over. Except when you feel these symptoms, try to avoid eating between meals, since it throws off the appetite control center of your brain that tells you when you need to eat, not just when you want to.

Many good nutritional cookbooks are available. Three worth having are *The American Heart Association Cookbook*, *The Athlete's Cookbook*, and *Laurel's Kitchen: A Handbook For Vegetarian Cookery and Nutrition*.[10]

Want to control your appetite and food consumption?

Do your aerobic exercise shortly before a meal, preferably lunch or dinner. Or, fifteen minutes before a meal, just take a walk. Exercise suppresses appetite.

Eat an apple, a slice of whole wheat bread or something else with high fiber, and drink two large glasses of water fifteen minutes before eating. The fiber absorbs the water and makes you feel full much faster. In fact, drinking six to eight large glasses of water per day curtails food cravings and cleans impurities out of your body.

Eat at a leisurely pace. Our fast food mentality often carries over to homemade dinners as well. We tend to see meals as a necessary interlude between the real activities of life. We've got things to do, places to go, people to see, so we wolf down our food. This hurried pace increases our stress levels, makes our digestive system work overtime to digest barely chewed food, and makes us eat more because the body can't say "I'm full" fast enough to stop us from eating more.

Chew your food slowly and thoroughly. Put down your fork between bites. Relax. Enjoy the food and the company of your family and friends. When you eat alone, read, and you'll eat slower and probably less.

Don't shop for groceries when you're hungry. This will not only leave you with less food crying out to be eaten, but it will save you lots of money!

Don't let your rule be "Eat everything on your plate," but "Put less on your plate." Take small portions, and leave yourself the option of seconds. The best way to eat less is to cook less. Food is wasted not by leaving it on the plate but by making too much of it. Remember, too, that food eaten in excess is more wasteful than food thrown away.

Help your children to take moderate helpings and not snack too much; then you won't lead them toward obesity by making them eat when they're not hungry. (One of our favorite lines was a mother saying to her five-year-old, "Eat all your Jell-O [82% sugar] or you can't have dessert.")

Say "no" to your appetite in order to tame it. Ultimately, whether or not you curb your appetite, you must control your consumption. Indulge your stomach like a spoiled child when it growls, whines, nags, and throws tantrums, and it will keep coming back for more.

Whether it's cocaine or chocolate, tranquilizers or potato chips, addictions are always reinforced—never overcome—

through surrender. Whether you are fat or skinny, gluttony—eating too much—is a sin (Proverbs 23:2, 20, 21; Philippians 3:19).

Don't go on starving binges. We all know the danger of eating binges. But binges of not eating are equally devastating to the body. Rely on exercise, not on starving yourself, to properly regulate your body weight. Otherwise, when the diet is over you'll regain the weight. The question is not what you managed to get by on in a brief burst of will power, but what you will be eating day in and day out the rest of your life. Remember that proper exercise and proper nutrition, not going hungry, are the keys to long-term weight control.

FEEDING YOUR FAMILY RIGHT

To some the nutritional guidelines of this chapter will seem restrictive and stifling. "What's left to eat?" The answer is, almost everything that hasn't been tampered with! If you take it on as a challenge, eating right is ultimately fun and liberating. Most supermarkets, not just health food stores, are now carrying good food (they still have the bad, so be careful).

If you have a family, all this is for their benefit as well. Men have a much greater chance of a heart attack from high fat consumption than women do. Overweight children are much more likely than others to develop heart disease when they become adults. A five-year study of sixteen hundred children ages five to twelve years clearly demonstrated that heart disease can and does begin in children.[11] What they eat now will affect their health the rest of their lives.

Let's reduce our stress by eating right!

FOOD FOR THOUGHT AND DISCUSSION

1. Can a person's eating habits relate in any way to her walk with Christ? (See 1 Corinthians 6:19-20). Explain.

2. Are you aware of any differences in yourself or your children

after consuming lots of sugar, caffeine or junk food? If so, what are they?

3. Are you happy with your own nutritional habits? How about your family's?

4. Which of the following areas would you like to see changed (increased or decreased) in your or your family's diet?

Sugar	Fruits	Vegetables
Fiber	Fat	Red meats
Salt	Caffeine	Whole Grains

5. What is the greatest obstacle to eating the way you should?

6. If you've tried to improve your or your family's nutrition in the past, what benefits have you seen as a result?

7. "The best reason I can think of for establishing and maintaining good eating habits is_____
_____."

1. Richard E. Ecker, *The Stress Myth* (Downer's Grove, Ill.: InterVarsity Press, 1985), p. 126.

2. Richard E. Ecker, *Staying Well* (Downer's Grove, Ill.: InterVarsity Press, 1984), p. 46.

3. Keith W. Sehnert, *Stress/Unstress* (Minneapolis: Augsburg Publishing House, 1981), p. 161.

4. Sugar Scoreboard Chart (Washington, D.C.. Center for Science in the Public Interest, 1985).

5. David Reuben, *The Save Your Life Diet* (New York: Ballantine Books, 1976), pp. 5-10.

6. Nathan Pritikin, *The Pritikin Permanent Weight Loss Manual* (New York: Bantam Books, 1981).

7. Ecker, *Staying Well*, p. 41.

8. Christine Ann Leatz, *Unwinding* (Englewood Cliffs, NJ: Prentice-Hall, 1981), p. 64.

9. "Vitamins: When More Is Too Much," *Changing Times*, April 1986, p. 45.

10. Mary Winston and Ruthe Eshelman, eds., *The American Heart Association Cookbook*, 3d ed. (New York: David McKay Co., 1979); Marilyn S. Peterson and Charlene Martinsen, *The Athlete's Cookbook* (Seattle: Smuggler's Cove, 1980); Laurel Robertson, *Laurel's Kitchen: A Handbook for Vegetarian Cookery and Nutrition* (New York: Bantam Books, 1978).

11. Steve Findlay, "Kids: Stay Thin Now, Save Hearts Later," *USA Today*, 26 July 1985, 1A.

12

YOUR HEALTH
AND YOUR HORMONES

DRUGS

Three years ago June had a back injury and started taking medication. Her back is better, but she now takes three medications—one to get her to sleep, one to get her going in the morning, and one to calm her down when she's under stress. "I think these drugs are causing more stress than they relieve," June admitted. "I know I should cut back, but every time I try I feel miserable."

The three best-selling prescription drugs in America are a tranquilizer (Valium), a heart drug (Inderal) and an ulcer medication (Tagamet). Twenty billion dollars a year is spent on prescription drugs in the United States. This includes over five billion dollars of tranquilizers alone, the great majority of which are taken by women.

"Take a Valium and get a good night's rest" is no doubt good advice on occasion, but it is not the cure-all it's often thought to be. Taken indiscriminately, medications can create as many problems as they solve.

Amphetamines and barbiturates are part of the regular diets of many Americans. Amphetamines are commonly taken to relieve fatigue and reduce weight. Because they stimulate the stress response, with its adrenaline production, they normally create fatigue in the long run. Furthermore, to get down from their effects, tranquilizers and sleeping pills are often prescribed. To get up from those, it's back to amphetamines. This up and down roller coaster is the ailment not simply of street people and wayward youths, but of a great many Christian women, such as our friend June.

Many non-prescription drugs are close relatives of amphetamines: they either imitate adrenaline or increase its production in the body. Among those are diet drugs such as Dexatrim, Appedrine, and Dietac, and cold formulas such as Sudafed, Dristan, Contac, Sinutab, and Allerest. Taken occasionally, these medications can be safe and helpful. Taken frequently over long periods they are highly addictive, stressful, and potentially harmful.

The most over-prescribed drugs are tranquilizers. Again, they can be very helpful in some situations, but be careful. You are ultimately responsible for what goes into your body. A doctor is a highly trained professional, but he is neither omniscient nor infallible, nor does he pretend to be.

Anti-depressant drugs are often prescribed by psychiatrists. This is certainly appropriate when the source of depression is chemical. But it is normally not an appropriate solution to "the blues," to depression rooted in wrong thinking, and to natural processes such as grief that must be worked through to be resolved.

Drugs can numb our brains, but they do not change our circumstances, our beliefs, our values, or any of the factors that determine correct thinking and proper perspective. In fact, sometimes they actually interfere with these, and draw attention from the need to develop long-term coping skills rather than short-term drug-induced escape. Use medications if needed, but use them wisely.

HEALTH CARE

In recent years there has been a movement toward a deeper understanding of total health care. Here are some important principles that need to be emphasized:

True health involves the total person, not just the body. Our society has emphasized the physical and neglected the spiritual. On the other hand, the church has too often de-emphasized the physical. Total health involves the total person—physical, mental and emotional, and spiritual.

Health is more than the absence of disease. It is the presence of a positive and mature frame of mind that fosters good self-care and sustains us as we deal with medical problems.

Many diseases—even some that can't be cured—can be prevented. More emphasis needs to be put on health education and the cultivation of personal and familial habits and lifestyles that prevent disease. Too often these habits and lifestyles are only implemented after the stroke or heart attack or cancer diagnosis. If people keep falling off a cliff, doesn't it make more sense to concentrate on putting railings at the top than stationing ambulances at the bottom?

The individual (assuming he is able to care for himself)—not the state, the doctor, or medical science—is ultimately responsible for his own health. Studies indicate that we bring on ouselves more than 90 percent of our ailments.[1] Some of these we can reverse, many we can control, most we can prevent. We must stop looking at doctors and medical science as an after-the-fact cure-all.

YOU AND YOUR DOCTOR

"My doctor has really let me down," Karen confided. "In the past he's always known what to do to make me feel better, but this time nothing he's doing is working. I don't understand why he can't help me."

Physicians, psychologists, and pastors share a lot in common (income is not what I have in mind). All three are trained and trusted authority figures. People entrust their bodies to physicians, their minds to psychologists, and their spirits to pastors.

And therein lies the problem.

Many people—and by our observation, especially many women—lay unrealistic expectations on all of these professionals. They go to their doctor to be made well, their psychologist to be made happy, and their pastor to be made spiritual.

But my doctor is not responsible for my physical health any more than my pastor is for my spiritual health. The moment I consider someone else to be responsible for me I am essentially considering myself to be non-responsible, which leads to being irresponsible. Now I don't have to really take care of myself, because my doctor can always make me better.

Every three months I see my doctor concerning my diabetes. She taught me how to give insulin injections and blood tests, she takes my readings, and answers a lot of my questions. She is very knowledgeable and helpful. But it is I, not she, who must control my diet, get my exercise and experience the rewards of right choices and the consequences of wrong ones. Helpful as my doctor is, she cannot live my life for me.

Furthermore, like psychologists and pastors, physicians are

only human. They are limited in knowledge and skills and are capable of making serious mistakes.

Realizing both the great value and the limitations of doctors, here are some guidelines to get the most benefit from them:

Ask the opinions of other people when choosing a doctor. Talk to those you trust. Is this doctor professional? Is he personal? Is he knowledgeable? Is he communicative?

Be sure your doctor is an expert in your particular area of need. Medical science is an incredibly broad and ever-growing field (in fact it is hundreds of fields under one gigantic umbrella). No doctor, no matter how knowledgeable and studious, can possibly be on the cutting edge of all medical research and developments. When necessary, most family practitioners will refer you to a specialist, but don't hesitate to ask for a referral.

Study up on health care. A good bookstore will carry several large illustrated home medical guides that cost less than a single doctor's appointment. Invest in one. Take a class. Watch health documentaries. Become informed.

Come to your doctor's appointment prepared and attentive. Have an accurate family history, list of medications, and copies of charts and X rays from other physicians. List your symptoms and write out your questions before your appointment, and go through each of them with your doctor. Summarize what you think he's said, and ask if you've understood him correctly.

Don't be a passive patient. If you don't understand what your doctor says, tell him. Ask him to rephrase, clarify, and elaborate. Take notes on what he says. When he sees you doing this, he's liable to say more and to say it more carefully. While you're at it, ask him to recommend some good literature. If you're nervous, bring a friend with you to your appointment. She can remind you of questions and help you sort out afterward what was and wasn't said.

If it is important, and especially if it involves a surgery, go to another doctor for a second opinion. Many insurance companies pay for the second opinion and some, in certain cases, require it. Asking for a second opinion is not an affront to your doctor—it demonstrates only a genuine concern for the proper stewardship of your health and your finances. No legitimate doctor will resist or resent a second opinion. On the contrary, he will welcome it, recommend it, and sometimes insist upon it.

Remember, your health is your responsibility. Go to your doctor, but don't expect him to take care of you. Take care of yourself.[2]

DEALING WITH DISEASES

When Dorothy was diagnosed as having Parkinson's disease, her world fell apart. In fact, her response to the disease was more disabling than the disease itself. Diseases not only bring their own stress, but often trigger potent stress responses.

There are many types of diseases. Some have purely organic roots. They may be triggered by genetic factors, an infection, or an accident. There are also imaginary diseases, which exist only in the mind. Other diseases are *psychosomatic*. Contrary to popular belief, psychosomatic diseases are not imaginary. They are real physical diseases involving actual tissue damage, nerve damage, chemical imbalances, etc. It is the mind and emotions (psyche) that cause these problems in the body (soma). Some physical problems can be entirely or largely attributed to mental and emotional conditions such as anger, worry, fear, and other stress-inducing states of mind.

Diseases are a fact of life in this imperfect world. Here are some suggestions to help you cope with them:

Mentally prepare yourself for the possibility of disease. It is probable that at some point in your life you will experience a fairly serious disease. One of three persons will eventually have some kind of cancer. One in five people, and more than one in three women, will eventually contract diabetes (in most cases, Type II diabetes). Usually these diseases can be effectively treated and adjusted to.

Become informed about your disease. Take an interest in what's going on in your body. Read widely. Talk to experts. Become an expert. There are foundations and support groups that disseminate information about almost every disease. Go to some classes and get on some mailing lists. Like difficult people, once you get to know a disease you find it much easier to live with.

Don't become preoccupied with your disease. I learn what I need to learn about my diabetes and do what I need to do, then I try to forget about it. There's a danger in thinking and talking too much about our health problems. If we always remind others of our diseases, they'll always remind us.

Make every effort to control your disease. Usually there is a pre-scribed regimen to follow that will help you control your dis-ease. Follow that regimen. Don't be one of those people who pretends she doesn't have a disease and ends up making it worse.

Look at the positive side of your disease. Yes, there is a positive side, as we saw in chapter four. One of the most godly women we know got that way through having a brain tumor and facing the likelihood of death. We know dozens of others with similar experiences, and you probably do too.

Since getting diabetes I take better care of my health, exer-cise more diligently, eat better, relax more, keep a saner schedule, have more time with my family, possess a better un-derstanding of others, am closer to God, and generally just enjoy life more (not bad, huh?). I know many others who likewise wouldn't trade what they've learned through their dis-ease and disabilities for anything. Like all stressors, seen through the eyes of faith, diseases can be stepping-stones to growth.

PMS AND MENOPAUSE

"Three times in the last three months I've felt so frustrated and depressed I've almost quit my job and left my family—but a few days later I've always felt fine again. I felt like a schizo, so I went to a counselor. When she asked me to pinpoint these times on the calendar, I realized that all three happened just a few days before my period started. Do you think they could be re-lated?"

In a word, yes.

Before we go further, can we suggest something to married women?

We think your husband could benefit by reading this book. But even if he reads nothing else, we recommend that you ask him to read this section.

Men, we encourage you to take a careful look at the things we will say here about PMS and menopause. Every attempt at using logic to change your wife's feelings during these times is bound to fail. What she needs from you is not logic, but empathy and help. If she knows that you know she is experiencing something real—that she is not making it up or going insane or just being a "weak woman"—it will be of tremendous encouragement to her.

By learning about these important parts of her life you can more readily obey God's command to "be considerate as you live with your wives, and treat them with respect" (1 Peter 3:7).

PRE-MENSTRUAL SYNDROME

Pre-menstrual syndrome (PMS) is the latest medical term for what women have said for millenia. "I get moody near my period." Here's what women—and men—need to know about PMS.

PMS is a reality. It is not an imaginary disorder. Certainly it can be blamed for too much, but it can and has been blamed for too little. A variety of major studies have been conducted to determine the physical and psychological effects of menstruation. While the results vary considerably, all of them reflect the fact that in many women menstruation is a major stressor.[3]

The hormones estrogen and progesterone drop off radically as menstruation approaches and stay at low levels till it passes. Many women tend to be emotionally down when these hormones drop, then experience a mood pick-up when they rise. The following chart illustrates this.[4]

Estrogen_____ Progesterone _ _ _ _ _ _ Mood ▬▬▬

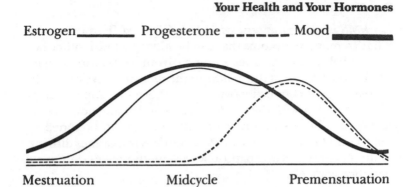

Mestruation   Midcycle   Premenstruation

While Nanci does not have severe PMS, we have often seen its effects. She is normally very easygoing and not at all oversensitive. But once in a while she will get very sensitive for no apparent reason. Invariably within a day she starts her period. This is not power of suggestion, because she often forgets when her period is supposed to come and it frequently comes several days early.

PMS has a large variety of symptoms that differ in intensity from woman to woman. Often there is a general feeling of loss of control. The most common specific symptoms are irritability, tension, moodiness, sensitivity, headaches, depression, fatigue, cramps, swelling and tenderness of breasts, bloated stomach, weight gain (usually water weight that is subsequently lost), increased thirst or appetite, acne, breathing difficulties, constipation, and cravings for sweet or salty foods.[5]

Of course, none of these symptoms necessarily indicates PMS (if they do, then I've had it). But when one or more of them occurs on a monthly cycle, they are likely to be linked to PMS.

Certain factors contribute to more severe PMS. According to a prominent PMS researcher, the more childbirths a woman has, the more severe her PMS will tend to be; married women complain more of PMS than single women; the closer to menopause, the more severe PMS tends to be (most common in women in their thirties); stress intensifies PMS; poor eating habits (specifically, high intake of refined sugar, salt, coffee, tea, chocolate, soft drinks and processed foods) magnify PMS symptoms; lack of outdoor exercise worsens PMS.[6]

PMS is often misunderstood and misdiagnosed. This is because it has so many symptoms that can be identified with other factors, and because it varies so much from woman to woman. PMS may come on in the middle of the menstrual cycle so there is no apparent connection with it. Furthermore, some doctors are not familiar with the recent research indicating not only the reality but the commonness of PMS. This is compounded by the fact that most doctors are male and it is sometimes difficult to understand and sympathize with something you cannot experience yourself.

PMS needs to be understood, accounted for, and adjusted to. Each woman tends to have her own pattern, and you can often learn to anticipate and mitigate the effects of your PMS. Prepare yourself by getting more rest, by not taking on extra responsibilities, and by being careful to apply the stress-reducing advice of this book, especially that related to exercise, nutrition and relaxation. Husbands, we can help in practical ways by taking care of the kids, doing the dishes, taking our wives out to dinner, and being especially patient if they experience mood swings.

PMS can cause needless guilt. The sensitive conscience of the Christian woman condemns her for being irritable, depressed, and weak. She may tell herself, and others may tell her, to "get it together" or, in essence, "be a man"—which is precisely the problem, since men do not have menstrual cycles. If they did, they would have more pronounced mood swings themselves.

We can't prove it, but we suspect that the menstrual cycle is one part of a woman's makeup which leads Peter to refer to her as the "weaker partner" (1 Peter 3:7). Not inferior, but different, she is often physically and emotionally more fragile (she also tends to be more sensitive and compassionate). Is her husband to look down on her for being the weaker partner? On the contrary, he is exhorted to "be considerate" and treat her "with respect" because she is a fellow heir of God's grace. Though different, she is his total spiritual equal.

When you've got the PMS blues, take care of yourself without coddling yourself. Don't make excuses, but don't be hard on yourself either. When you think no one understands, remember that God does. He made that body of yours and he knows its nature and its frailties. God is kind to you. So be kind to yourself. (Also, be aware that if PMS becomes a serious problem, medical treatment may be possible—ask your family practitioner's advice and he may refer you to a specialist.)

MENOPAUSE

Sally is forty-four, a normally cheerful and upbeat school teacher with the rare knack of getting along well with seventh graders. But last year Sally's menopause began, and with it a personality change that is all too obvious to her friends, students, and colleagues. She is uncharacteristically moody and impatient, especially with her students. For the first time in twenty years of teaching she lost her temper and yelled at her class. Sally knew "the change" was coming, but she was totally unprepared for its far-reaching effects.

Menopause is the stage in a woman's life when her ovaries stop producing estrogen, the primary female hormone. This eventually brings ovulation to a halt and terminates the entire menstrual cycle. Menopause is the phasing out of a woman's reproductive system.

When does this happen? Often in her forties (but sometimes as early as her thirties or as late as her fifties) a woman's menstrual cycle may begin to get shorter, as short as twenty days. Some cycles may be missed while others are longer than normal. Sometimes the cycles have a clear beginning but not a clear ending.

Usually between the ages of forty-five and fifty-five (fifty to fifty-one is the average) her periods will stop completely.[7] This, technically, is the point of menopause. However, the term menopause is often used more broadly to describe this whole season of a woman's life.

Menopause has some of the same symptoms as PMS, but they are not as cyclical and they may be more intense and last over a period of years. Menopause can precipitate headaches, fatigue, dizziness, nausea, and insomnia. It often involves hot flashes followed by a flushing of the face, sweating, and shivering. Though they are linked somehow to low estrogen, research has still not determined the exact cause of menopausal hot flashes.[8]

Other physical symptoms of menopause may be dry skin, reduced sexual desire, weight loss, pain in the joints, and in some cases osteoporosis. In his excellent chapter on menopause, Dr. James Dobson states that one of the most common and telling symptoms of estrogen deprival is dark gloomy circles around the eyes.[9]

Menopause may bring on irritability, anxiety, depression, and fearfulness. Crying spells are common, as is sensitivity to noises, low tolerance of others, flaring temper, and mental lapses.

The symptoms of menopause commonly occur over a three to seven year period. While most women adjust to this transition into life's autumn, some go into a nose dive. These women may be not only fatigued, but exhausted. They may be immersed in a fog of fear and in free-floating anxiety. Even routine tasks become very difficult for them. They may feel their mental capacities are dwindling, that they are rapidly becoming senile and useless.

INSIDE THE HEAD OF THE MENOPAUSAL WOMAN

Menopause is often accompanied by a severe decline in self-esteem. This sometimes relates to a woman's feeling that she is being defeminized. Before menopause this woman may not have wanted to have more children, but now she *cannot* have them, and the impact of this may be devastating.

Menopause is change, and all change brings stress. It commonly involves grief and depression due to an acute sense of loss. A woman is losing something which, though she may have cursed it, has been with her since she made the transition from being a girl to a woman. Her period has symbolized her youthfulness and her femininity. Menopause is a symbol of something else—age and mortality.

It is at about this same time that she is getting crow's feet, more and more wrinkles, and losing the bounce in her step.

Her hair may be graying and thinning, her pants fitting tighter. Even if she says nothing about it to anyone, she is all too aware that these things are happening.

Menopause is compounded by the fact that it usually comes at a time when a mother is facing the empty nest. After twenty-five years of childraising she is suddenly out of a job. Her children are grown and she feels they no longer need her. Or, her remaining children are teenagers, struggling with rebellion and rejection that require from mom extra energy, patience, and a good self-image—which right now are in short supply.

Meanwhile, the typical menopausal woman's husband is at the peak of his career. While she is getting older, he is getting "more distinguished." He's busy being successful without her. His job may be the "other woman." But there may also be a literal "other woman." After all, young women who work around him may be attracted to him, and he to them. What competition is she (so she thinks) for working girls in their twenties and thirties?

She may spend hours alone, feeling lonely, unwanted and unneeded, becoming self-absorbed, imagining and expecting the worst (and in the process sometimes bringing it on). She may give up on herself, turn to alcohol and overeating, waste away her days watching game shows and soap operas. Mid-life would be hard enough for a woman without menopause. Yet at this time of life when a woman is most in need of love, she may be feeling her most unlovable.

In addition to everything else, her husband may be facing his own mid-life crisis (sometimes—misleadingly—called "male menopause"). This couple needs each other's strength more than ever, yet both may be too preoccupied with their own needs to meet the other's.

Meanwhile this woman's parents are aging. She knows eventually she will lose them. Perhaps she is now making difficult decisions about whether to bring them in to live with her, or to help them find a retirement home.

The woman in menopause has until recently thought of herself as being young rather than middle-aged. But subtle hints from her high schoolers remind her otherwise. "Mom, to-morrow's Nerd Dress Up Day—can we borrow some of your clothes?"

The menopausal mother hears the ticking of the clock. Known to others as "Dave's wife" or "Susie's mom," she may step out in a restless—perhaps even reckless—pursuit of herself. She may subconsciously be looking for one last chance to prove she still has something to offer. Perhaps she starts working outside the home for the first time, goes back to college, loses weight, buys a new wardrobe, finds new friends. Sometimes this is good. Other times it leads to a superficial basis for her self-esteem, a fragmented marriage, and even an affair or divorce.

The woman who married young, moving straight from under her father's authority to her husband's, may find herself resenting men in general and her husband in particular. First she was daughter, then wife, then mother. Now she wants to be herself.

Of course, some women make a smooth transition through menopause and into mid-life. If you do, be thankful. If you don't, remind yourself that menopause is a God-ordained season of your life. Commit yourself to drawing on his strength and perspective to make the very best of it.

Here are some important things to know about menopause and mid-life:

Menopause is a physical and chemical reality. The production of the hormone estrogen is severely diminished at this stage in a woman's life (her body may produce about 15 percent of what it did in previous years). While there are various psychological responses to menopause, menopause itself is not psychological or in any sense imaginary. It eventually happens to every woman.

Many things about menopause are unpredictable. You know it will come, but not exactly when and not exactly how. It varies in its nature and intensity from woman to woman. As in PMS, there are hereditary factors involved. If your mother and grandmother had similar menopausal experiences there is a

218

good chance yours will be like theirs. One study indicates that 50 percent of women adjust well to menopause, 40 percent adjust to it with greater difficulty, and 10 percent have major problems adjusting.

Most women are not prepared for menopause. It is interesting and curious that in light of the universal certainty of menopause, relatively little is said to prepare most women for it. Perhaps, like death, we subconsciously (and irrationally) feel that thinking about it will bring it on sooner or somehow make it worse. On the contrary, knowing what to expect and ways to cope with it can greatly reduce the stresses of menopause.

We urge you to read up on menopause (a good bookstore will have several resources on the subject). The more you know in advance, the more prepared and the less stressed you will be when you experience menopause.

Most women who have a difficult menopause can be greatly helped medically. If menopause is giving you fits, by all means see a doctor. If he doesn't seem to understand menopause or your symptoms, go to someone else. If you know of a good female gynecologist, go to her—especially if she's in her forties or older. She'll probably know exactly what you're talking about!

Estrogen or progesterone therapy, or a combination of both, can often be very effective in helping women through menopause. It is true that estrogen therapy can involve some risks and side effects, most notably raised blood pressure and increased risk of endometrial cancer. But these risks are sometimes more than compensated for by the benefits. Some women are helped by taking estrogen just long enough to get them through the transition period. Their dosage can then taper off. Talk to your doctor about this, and be sure to get a second opinion.

You will emerge on the other side of menopause. Expect the transition period, be prepared for the transition period, but above all, hang on during the transition period. It may be easier than you think or it may be harder than you think, but you *will* make it through.

All of this is not to suggest that during menopause life need be miserable and that the best you can hope for is survival! It is only to say that at times menopause may seem like a very dark tunnel. Look for the light at the end of that tunnel. Even better, look for the light *in* the tunnel, realizing that Jesus promises to be with you every step along the way (Matthew 28:20).

Here are some things you can do about menopause:

Remind yourself of the true basis of your personal identity. Who you are is rooted in Christ and who he has made you, not in your outward appearance or performance. Rehearse the fact that the most important part of your life is the part that only God sees. His deepest concern is about the inner you. True beauty is inner beauty, and it does not diminish but deepens as you grow older.

If you don't already have special interests, hobbies, and activities, develop them. Get involved. Be active. Use both your mind and your body. Take up golf, read a novel, write a novel, learn to paint, develop your skills as a photographer. Travel and sightsee.

Cultivate friendships and reach out in ministry to others. As you meet their needs God will meet yours. "It is more blessed to give than to receive" (Acts 20:35).

Look at the positive side of growing older. First, realize that fifty isn't old, neither is sixty, and seventy and eighty don't have to be either. Your mindset is much more important than your age. But if God keeps you here long enough to really get old, then be grateful you've lived so long! And determine to enjoy every day, month, and year that God gives you. Remember, he wouldn't have you here if there wasn't a purpose.

Most societies venerate the elderly. Think of the experience and wisdom the older person has gained in all her years of life. She has so much to offer others. I love to be around older people—that is, older people who have sweetened with age, not those who have soured. As you get older are you sweetening or souring? The choice is yours.

You can be one of those godly old saints people love to be around. The more you've walked with the Lord the more you'll have to offer your children, grandchildren, great-grandchildren, friends, neighbors, and church family.

I won't pretend that growing old is easy. It isn't. But there is still something beautiful about it for the Christian. There are always people to share your life with—people to help and people to help you. And with you is your God, who knew you before birth and will take you through death to the glory of his presence. Robert Browning's words can be applied to our relationships with our loved ones and with God:

> Grow old with me;
>   the best is yet to be.
> The last of life,
>   for which the first was made.

FOOD FOR THOUGHT AND DISCUSSION

1. "Medications and drugs can have an appropriate and helpful place in our lives, but we must be very careful how we use them." Agree or disagree? If you can, give an example of the proper use and the abuse of medications.

2. Respond to this statement: "The individual (assuming he is able to care for himself)—not the state, the doctor, or medical science—is ultimately responsible for his own health."

3. Do you think we sometimes place unrealistic expectations on doctors? If so, can you think of an example?

4. Do you or does someone close to you have a disease or disorder? How does it affect you/them? What have you/they learned about how to cope with it?

5. Have you experienced any of the symptoms of PMS? What effect do you feel your monthly cycle has on your own physical, mental, and emotional state of being?

   none   a little   considerable   extreme

6. Do you think that in the past the reality of PMS has been denied, ignored, or overlooked? If so, why?

7. Have you ever experienced guilt feelings because of moodiness or irritability that might be related to PMS or menopause? What self-talk would you prescribe to help you deal with these guilt feelings?

8. "Menopause is not only a difficult experience in itself, but it often comes at a difficult point in a woman's life." Agree or disagree? Why?

9. A Christian woman you know is having a hard time coping with her menopause. What can you say or do to help her?

1. Keith W. Sehnert, *Selfcare/Wellcare* (Minneapolis.. Augsburg, 1985), p. 17.

2. As a basic, practical, and helpful guide to self-care that includes an alphabetic listing of health problems and what you can do about them, we recommend Keith W. Sehnert's *SelfCare/ Wellcare* (Minneapolis: Augsburg, 1985).

3. Barbara Sommer, "Stress and Menstrual Distress," *Journal of Human Stress,* September 1978.

4. "Normal Hormone Levels and Mood" chart from James Dobson's *What Wives Wish Their Husbands Knew about Women* (Wheaton, Ill.: Tyndale House, 1975), p. 151. Used by permission.

5. Ronald V. Norris and Colleen Sullivan, *PMS* (New York: Berkley Books, 1983), pp. 3-4.

6. Guy E. Abraham, *Premenstrual Blues* (Rolling Hills, Calif.: Optimox Co., 1982).

7. Norris and Sullivan, p. 180.

8. Ibid., p. 182.

9. Dobson, p. 148.

13

DISCOVERING THE LOST ART OF RELAXATION

"**R**elax! How can I relax? My life is an endless string of responsibilities. It's been years since I've been able to relax."

To some, the word *relaxation* evokes thoughts of peace and well-being. To others it conjures up nothing but guilt feelings. We are so caught up with commitments, obligations, responsibilities, duties, and tasks—most of which we won't ever really finish—that relaxing seems a synonym for irresponsibility, neglect, and laziness.

Ironically, the woman who doesn't take time to relax (we must *take* time, we will never find it), cheats not only herself but her loved ones and her Lord—all in the name of being responsible. Unless she allows her energy reservoir to fill up through regular times of relaxation, she will be drawing from its sludgy bottom until it dries up entirely.

The same women who feel guilty if they do relax, end up feeling resentful if they don't. At first they pour themselves out unceasingly. Then one day they wake up to the realization that no self is left to pour out, or the ragged self that is left is not the self they want to be. These women get scared, desperate, and often angry and bitter. The family they slaved for, they suddenly resent.

THE IMPORTANCE OF RELAXATION

Like jackrabbits on a hot tin roof, some of us are never still—always doing, always going. We strive to justify our worth by creating motion. Do the laundry, plant the flowers, wash the floor, attend the meeting, make the phone call, plan the dinner . . . all worthwhile activities *if* we stop long enough to breathe and think and grow and relax.

Paradoxically, in an age where we have more leisure time we are leisurely about little. We busily pursue our leisure time activities, turning play into work. We don't let ourselves really play the way we did when we were kids. Remember how hours at a time were lost in the joy of being alive and discovering trees and trails and caterpillars and the new friend on the block? We didn't justify playing. It was its own justification.

But even on a rare day of leisure time, today's woman might rush to the spa to relax in a whirlpool, then rush to a restaurant to enjoy a lunch, then rush to the shopping mall to fight through the crowd to the great sale. We are tyrannized by the ticking of the clock. We frantically wrestle with life instead of sitting back to enjoy it.

Even our vacations are planned with the precision of a military maneuver (men are particularly guilty here). "We'll relax and have fun beginning tomorrow morning at 6:00 A.M. when we pack the car and hit the freeway. We will then drive five hundred miles, stopping only for gas, food, and emergency bladder failures, and we will make every effort to synchronize these events." And we wonder why we and the kids get cranky on vacations!

We can't overemphasize that feeling guilty about relaxing is self-defeating.

The automaker never intended the car to run day and night, accelerator to the floor. Your Maker never intended you to go nonstop either. In fact, one of the Ten Commandments—right up there with no false gods, no murder, and no adultery—is a divine mandate to quit working and get regular rest (Exodus 20:8-11). God doesn't just permit or recommend rest—he commands it. Refusing to relax is not only unhealthy, it's disobedient.

Relax. And relax in the knowledge that doing so is God's very best for you and your family.

REDISCOVERING THE OUTDOORS

One giant step in discovering how to relax is the step out your door. Yet, most of us spend the majority of our lives indoors. Our outdoor time consists of walking from house to car and car to office or store or school. Six months of the year or more, our outdoor living takes place primarily in parking lots.

Two of the Great Physician's effective therapeutic treatments are the sun and the air. Sun rays produce vitamin D in the body, helping it to assimilate calcium, which has a proven effect of calming the body. It is typical of our artificial age conclude that all we need to do, therefore, is take vitamin D and calcium pills (and maybe lie under a sun lamp) for the same effect. But the physical and especially the psychological benefits of experiencing sunlight are inestimable. This is why many hospitals go to such expense to build solariums—to aid patients in their recovery from illness and surgeries. Research is now being done with "light boxes" that imitate sunlight for people confined to the indoors. Some chronically depressed people are reporting dramatically improved dispositions as a result of a few hours exposure per day.

Both indoor living and our polluted environments discourage deep breathing. We learn to breathe shallowly, so just enough oxygen gets to our lungs to keep us alive, but not enough to really relax or invigorate us. Yet one of the most effective ways to relax and reduce stress is simply the deep breathing of fresh air.

Studies show there is a high correlation between indoor living and depression. As a counselor I noticed that the time of year when people suffer most from depression (and just about every other emotional disorder) is in the months of November through February. In fall and spring the requests for counseling were half of what they were in winter, and in the summer they were even less. (Certainly there are other factors that contribute to this phenomenon, but lack of regular exposure to sunlight and fresh air in the winter months is probably a major one.)

Most of us just need to get outdoors more. Make it part of your daily plan. Whether it's working in the garden, an outdoor quiet time, or a daily walk or run, get out and do something. It doesn't have to be a warm or cloudless day to benefit from sunlight or fresh air. Bundle up and take daily walks in the winter months. It won't hurt to get wet if you have the right clothing. If you're elderly or have been ill, get someone to walk with you. If you have children, take them with you.

If you're interested in hiking, backpacking, or skiing, they can be your ticket not only to exercise but relaxation. The psychological benefits of outdoor activities are just as significant as the physical benefits.

METHODS OF RELAXATION

There are certain things you can do to enhance your relaxation. Here are some specific techniques you may find helpful.

Stretching. Long periods of slow and deliberate stretching increase flexibility, decrease muscle soreness and the possibility of injury, improve coordination, and reduce muscular tension. A stretched-out body is the opposite of a tensed up body. Stretching is a great promoter of relaxation.

Stretching is of particular benefit before and after exercise, after prolonged sitting or standing, early in the morning, just before bed, and during any period of tension.

Proper stretching technique is gradual, relaxed, and sustained. Extend your stretch gradually with each repetition. Try to cover the major muscle groups. There are many ways to stretch. Buy a good stretching book with pictures or drawings or take a class on stretching (health clubs and community colleges frequently offer them.)

Stretching can be combined with deep breathing, biblical meditation and prayer, and relaxing music. Twenty minutes of stretching each day can do wonders for your body and mind.

Saunas, steam rooms, whirlpools, and warm baths. Heat enhances your circulation, draws blood to your extremities and your muscle tissues. It loosens up tight tense muscles. This physical relaxation in turn promotes mental and emotional relaxation. As physical tension is released, so is emotional anxiety.

Heating pads and heat ointments can be effective in reducing soreness and the tension it creates. Stiffness is often alleviated by alternating heat and cold applications. The warm bath or whirlpool are especially effective in decreasing soreness and stiffness and enhancing both the ability to get to sleep and the quality of sleep. (Usually you should not exceed a half hour of immersion in warm water.)

Because your feet are so important, a heated foot bath (some come with air jets) can be a very effective and reasonably priced tension-reducing option.

Massage. Massage is the manipulation of body tissues and muscle for remedial and relaxation purposes. Massage improves circulation and can reduce swelling and pain.

A good massage usually involves rubbing, stroking, or kneading. It is systematic, deliberate, and firm, moving from region to region across the body. Oils and powders are often used to make the stroking and kneading more smooth and relaxing. Massages can be given with the hands or a special instrument, such as a roller. A paint roller (preferably without the paint) is inexpensive and effective.

It is possible to give yourself local massage with your fingers and thumb. This can help a sore neck, shoulders, arms, legs, or feet. However, the most effective massage is done by another person who has been properly trained how and where to apply pressure. Having someone else do the massage allows the subject to stretch out completely and relax, which is impossible in self-massage. Furthermore, a critical massage area is the back, which can't be reached in self-massage.

Nanci and I took a course on full body massage offered by a hospital. We highly recommend it. Go to a class with your husband or a friend. It's good for your body and your relationship. (Nanci often massages the girls—it has a wonderfully calming effect on them and it's a great form of bonding.)

Deep breathing. This is a simple but extremely effective relaxation method. Assume a comfortable position. Dim the lights, close your eyes, and play soft music if you wish.

Inhale deeply through your nose (the fresher the air the better). Fill your lungs completely. This requires expanding your stomach. Exhale through your mouth. When you breathe out your stomach contracts. Breathe in and out slowly, from the diaphragm, not the upper lungs.

The increased oxygen intake is very healthy for the body. In fact whenever we yawn, our bodies are attempting to take in more oxygen. Some people induce their own yawns as a relaxation technique.

Good posture. This can preserve you from a lifetime of backaches, shoulder aches, and neck aches. Slumped shoulders are killers. Do you tend to hunch over the steering wheel, desk, table or stove? Straighten up and you'll reduce tension and prevent a lot of problems.

Getting comfortable. Much of our physical tension is needless. If you have to strain and wince to see something clearly, go to an optometrist and see if you need vision correction. If you have eyeglasses, be sure they're adjusted properly so that you don't have to tense up your facial muscles to hold them in place.

Choose comfortable furniture. The more time you spend sitting, the more critical your chair is. If your back aches, try the backless chairs that put the primary pressure on your legs.

Dim the lights. Blaring lights are hard on your eyes. You wince unknowingly, creating facial tension. Often when the lights are dim you can feel your face relax.

Tightly fitting clothes restrict blood flow and cause stomachaches, headaches, rashes and chafing, which in turn lead to irritability and tension. Shoes are particularly important. Our feet don't care what our shoes look like, just what they feel like. The stylishness of high heels is rarely worth the tension they inflict on your body.

When we're home by ourselves, Nanci and I have just a few favorite outfits we always wear. They are symbols of relaxation, and just putting them on actually helps us turn off our responsibilities. Even when we have to go out and look acceptable, we aim for comfort. Admittedly, we are jeopardizing our chances of making the cover of *Glamour* or *Gentleman's Quarterly*—but that's a price we're willing to pay for being comfortable.

Biofeedback. Contrary to what was thought for many years, it is now known that people can be taught to control such stress-related functions as their pulse, blood pressure, and even their brain waves. This control is the goal of biofeedback.

In biofeedback a patient may be connected to a machine with a monitor that indicates her blood pressure, the tension in her facial muscles, and/or the temperature of her fingers. The patient gets immediate feedback regarding her body's respons to her thoughts and actions. By utilizing relaxation skills learns to create and maintain the positive physical effects and avoid the negative ones.

Among other things, biofeedback has been very helpful in reducing the severity and frequency of migraine headaches. If you think you can be helped by biofeedback, contact a medical clinic in your area.

Professional biofeedback machinery is very expensive, but more reasonably priced home equipment is increasingly available. One of the simplest forms of biofeedback is the little card that you put on your finger for ten seconds (available in variety and book stores and in some medical clinics). It measures your skin temperature and turns a certain color to indicate your level of relaxation (the more tense you are the less blood flows to your extremities and therefore the colder your fingers). Another method is a small dot that you keep on your hand all day. By periodically checking its color, you see what degree of stress you are experiencing, are reminded to relax, and can see which attempts at relaxation work and which ones don't.

Avoiding noise. Have you noticed how you tense up when there's a loud noise? One study showed that people living near Los Angeles International Airport have measurably higher rates of hypertension, heart disease, and suicide than those living in quieter environments in the same city.[1] Another study measured the decibel level of common sounds and found that a crying baby held six inches from the ear creates an effectively higher noise level than standing beside a moving freight train.

Obviously, we can't always get away from noise. But we can cut out a lot of clatter, turn down the TV, and learn not to raise our voices. If you need to you can block outside noises with ear plugs or, more practically, with music.

Listening to relaxing music. Nothing can create or alleviate stress so effectively as what comes into our ears. The only thing that helped Saul come out of his depression was soft beautiful music (1 Samuel 16:23). We are very fortunate to have a wide variety of music at our disposal, as well as the equipment to play it with. Praise music and classical music are our favorite stress-relievers.

MENTAL VACATIONS

Relaxation is intended by God to be a regular part of our lives, a natural outlet for stress, and an inlet to renew energy.

Relaxation can be a coping strategy in which we tap the body's God-given ability to escape the fight or flight syndrome. When we relax we take ourselves out of gear, allowing ourselves to idle rather than race. Paradoxically, learning to relax requires some effort because tenseness has become the rule rather than the exception. Many of us have literally forgotten how to relax.

One of God's greatest gifts to us is our imagination. With it we can soar to places we once were or places we have never been. And we can learn to take mental vacations.

Get in a comfortable position, dim the lights, stretch out a little, breathe deeply and relax. Feel the tenseness drain from your head to your toes.

Now imagine a beautiful scene—perhaps a meadow, mountain, beach, or favorite childhood place. See the deep blue sky, white fluffy clouds, or the brilliant crimson of the sun setting between giant ocean rocks. Feel the mist on your face, the gentle wind, and the warmth of the sun's rays. Taste the salty air, smell the flowers or fallen leaves, pick up a beautiful rock or shell.

Perhaps you'd like to imagine the Lord Jesus sitting beside you or walking with you on the beach or in the meadow. Hear him speaking to you words of love and affirmation. This can be an intimate spiritual experience.

The physical and psychological benefits of taking mental vacations are inestimable. If it is difficult for you to do this at first, it's only because your imagination has become rusty through lack of use. Your imagination can get just the prompting it needs if you listen to the sounds of nature through stereo tapes of oceans, waterfalls, birds chirping, and other environmental delights.[2]

Medical science is discovering more and more about the power of the mind over the body. In fact, one radiologist has hi

c

cancer patients imagine their tumor cells being hunted down and devoured by defender cells that look like white knights. The result has been amazing—many terminally ill patients have survived beyond all expectations.[3]

PROGRESSIVE RELAXATION

One of the most proven ways to relax your body and mind is *progressive relaxation*, a process in which you first tense up, then release different body muscles from head to toe.

This technique can be practiced locally through taking a deep breath, then holding it in while making a fist for ten seconds, followed by breathing out and relaxing your hand. Through experiencing the contrast between tension and relaxation, your body can learn better to relax.

Another exercise is to sit upright on the edge of a straight chair, knees twelve inches apart, legs stretching forward (greater than 90 degrees). Suddenly let yourself collapse into the chair like a rag doll, so your head falls forward, your spine rounds, and your hands dangle.

You can buy progressive relaxation tapes or, as Nanci has done, you can make your own tape, going inch by inch down your body, telling yourself "My jaw is warm and heavy," "My jaw is loose, limp, and slack," "My shoulders are warm and heavy," "My shoulders are loose, limp, and slack." This is not hypnosis but it does create a relaxing mental state.

RELAXING THROUGH SLEEP

A godly Bible teacher was asked the key ingredient in his own life to walking in the Spirit. Of course, he studied God's word, prayed, and met with the Lord daily. But his surprising reply to the question was this: "Getting eight hours of sleep each night."

Sleep does indeed have a profound effect on every aspect of our being—physical, mental, emotional, and even spiritual. Sleep is the body's most basic and extensive attempt at relaxation and renewal. Stress often causes a lack of good sleep. Ironically, a lack of good sleep will inevitably cause stress.

It's easy to stay up late tonight, but tomorrow we, and those around us, will pay the price in the form of our fatigue and irritability. Often the key to the quality with which we experience today is what we did last night and how late we did it. Put two or three busy nights with six hours of sleep together and we're deep in debt, trying to spend energy we don't have.

It's a simple matter of mathematics. If I need eight hours of sleep and I must get up at 6:30 in the morning, then I need to be asleep at 10:30. Not heading for bed at 10:30, but asleep at 10:30, which probably means I should try to be in bed by 10:00. Which means I better leave my friend's house by 9:15, and I can't watch the evening movie.

Sonya is a woman we know who tries to sleep but can't. "I lie in bed eight or nine hours a night and sleep three or four, or even less." Insomnia can be maddening. Here's a number of suggestions that Sonya, we, and others have found helpful—perhaps you will, too.

Get a good mattress. If we will spend one-third of our lives in a bed, isn't it worth having a good one? Especially since the quality of that one-third will dramatically affect the other two-thirds. Many of us sleep better in a larger bed. Some find waterbeds far more restful then conventional ones.

Watch the room temperature and the ventilation. Too hot or too cold means sleeplessness or restless sleep. Adding or subtracting covers or adjusting an electric blanket may be enough to make the difference.

Some people need fresh air to sleep, so they crack the window even in winter. Try it. If the air is too dry for you, get a humidifier.

Minimize distractions. Are there street lights and traffic noises that disturb you? Perhaps you can move into a smaller bedroom at another end of the house. Or maybe you need to get very thick shades to keep out the light or a sleeping mask to cover your eyes or earplugs to keep out the noises.

Discovering the Lost Art of Relaxation

Relax before you get into bed. Many poor sleepers instinctively tighten up when they get into bed, ready for the big fight for sleep which they invariably lose. Instead of trying to relax once in bed, relax before you get there. Take a walk—get some fresh air. Take a warm bath to reduce your tension. Drink warm milk—it contains a natural tranquilizer.

Avoid chemical stimulants before going to bed. No caffeine within five hours and no chocolate or sugar of any kind within three hours of going to bed.

Eat an early dinner, moderately sized. If you eat a large dinner or a late dinner or a big snack at 8:00 P.M., your body is still trying to digest it when you go to bed. You can't give your body a chore to do, then expect it to sleep at the same time! On the other hand, if you eat like a bird you'll end up snacking or unable to sleep because of hunger pangs.

Avoid working on problems and reading or watching distressing things late at night. Don't try to balance your checkbook or do anything that requires deep thought late at night; it just causes frustration and leads to sleeplessness.

A few years ago I was at the beach by myself for ten days of writing. Each night I slept soundly and woke up refreshed—except one night when I was fitful and restless, and woke up exhausted. That one night was the only one I had watched the eleven o'clock news.

The single best cure for many people's insomnia is precisely that—never watch the late news. Why? It invariably features murders, hijackings, kidnappings, wars, and natural disasters. Just thinking of these things tightens us up, and whether we're conscious of them or not they keep us from sleeping. The same is true of watching violent or tense movies, or reading about distressing events in the newspaper just before going to bed. Our last dominant thoughts before the lights go out set the mood for our night's sleep. If you want good sleep, make sure you close the day with good thoughts.

Develop a bedtime ritual. We are creatures of habit. If we can associate sleep with a certain routine, then going through the routine can help induce sleep. A bedtime ritual might involve a warm bath, a cup of warm milk, soft music, or light reading. Some people read till they begin to nod off then turn off the light and go right to sleep.

If you just can't get an idea or problem off your mind, get up and do something about it. Sometimes we really need to get something off our minds. Keep paper and pen (and perhaps a little light) by your bed. If you need to, go through your bedtime ritual again to get to sleep.

Learn when to nap and when not to. There are two kinds of fatigue. *Hypertonic fatigue* is the nervous stress-induced fatigue in which you are tired but unable to relax. *Hypotonic fatigue* results from hard physical labor. The muscles are relaxed and the mind drifts quickly into sleep. If you experience hypertonic fatigue during the day, the best cure is exercise, not a nap. If you take a nap, it might not refresh you, but even if it does it will usually make it more difficult for you to sleep at night. (Sometimes this creates a vicious cycle in which you nap in the afternoon because you can't sleep at night, but can't sleep at night because you napped in the afternoon).

By all means, nap if your fatigue is hypotonic and especially if you have a big evening ahead of you. As long as you don't nap too long (an hour or less), chances are you'll still be able to sleep well tonight.

PERIODIC REST

God built our bodies and minds to require periodic rest. This is obviously true of the weekly day of rest that Scripture models and commands (Genesis 2:2, Exodus 20:8-11).

It is not our concern here to decide whether the day of rest should be one day as opposed to another, or exactly what can and can't be done on that day in our own era. But there is a timeless truth behind this command that is independent of the law given to Israel (Genesis 2:2 long preceded the law). The principle of a weekly day of rest does apply to us today. If we violate that principle we are bound to pay the price of physical, psychological, and spiritual depletion and stagnation.

"But what about when there is so much to do and you can't take a day off from all your work?" God anticipated that argument:

> Six days you shall labor, but on the seventh day you shall rest; even during the plowing season and harvest you must rest (Exodus 34:21).

After the apostles had gone out and ministered to people, they returned to Jesus, and Scripture gives us this account:

> The apostles gathered around Jesus and reported to him all they had done and taught. Then, because so many people were coming and going that they did not even have a chance to eat, he said to them, "Come with me by yourselves to a quiet place and get some rest."
>
> So they went away by themselves in a boat to a solitary place (Mark 6:30-32).

Jesus knew there was a time to work and a time to rest. He prescribed rest for his disciples knowing their needs even when they didn't, and knowing their long-range labors would only be enhanced by their short-range rest.

In Israel there was not only a weekly day of rest, but several yearly weeks of rest (feasts and celebrations), and every seven years an entire year of rest in which the land was not worked (Exodus 23:10-11, Leviticus 25:1-7, Nehemiah 10:31). Every fiftieth year was the year of Jubilee, in which debts were forgiven and family property was restored (Leviticus 25:8-13). So, both the forty-ninth and fiftieth years were taken off, a two year rest that most people would experience once in their lifetime.

This same principle of rest applies daily. Everyday we need to take an hour or two to refresh ourselves, to relax, to do as we wish. Part of that is your quiet time with God, part may be one of the diversions we'll talk about in a minute. Every week take a day with yourself, a friend, or your family—a day as much as possible without duties or obligations. Perhaps you can make a weekly exchange with a friend—you assume some of her responsibilities one day a week, and she assumes some of yours, freeing you up for the day.

DIVERSIONS, HOBBIES, AND SPECIAL INTERESTS

Everybody needs R & R (rest and relaxation). But what do you do with it? Just lay around?

Change your environment. Get outdoors more. Read a good book (if you're the practical sort, like me, indulge yourself in some fiction so you don't have to do anything but enjoy the story). Take a drive. Ride a bike. If it's fun for you, rearrange your furniture, bake bread, plant flowers. If that's work for you, forget it.

Play tennis. Sketch. Paint. Do stained glass work. Go to breakfast with a friend. Join a choir. Collect shells or rocks. Take up windsurfing. Ice skate. Bowl. Golf.

Bundle up on a clear night, lay down on a blanket and star gaze (use binoculars—they're great). Watch for meteorites and satellites. Take up photography. Go for a hike. Listen to the birds. Watch the chipmunks (use those binoculars again).

Go to the lake, the river, the beach. Wander through the shops. Browse in a book store. Give yourself a whole day to do whatever comes your way.

Plan your next vacation (it's as fun as going). Plan it with someone.

LIFE-GIVING LAUGHTER

Some Christians act like having fun is a sin. It isn't. But not having fun is a shame.

Kick up your heels. Give yourself permission to have fun. Laugh. We laugh together everyday, often hilariously. Sometimes we can't stop. Between us and the girls there's a lot of giggling and laughing and carrying on at the dinner table. Not laughter at another's expense, but the kind of laughter that draws people together. The friendships we enjoy most are the ones where we feel free to really laugh together. Seek out those kinds of friendships.

Our annual church retreat is the highlight of the year for many in our church family. On Saturday night we have our skit night, and the laughter is uproarious, contagious, and delightful. Every year the house comes down. (One retreat speaker told us his face literally ached the next morning from laughing so hard).

Norman Cousins gives an amazing account of laughter's therapeutic value in his book *Anatomy of an Illness*.[4] Diagnosed with an untreatable terminal disease, Cousins determined to cultivate a positive frame of mind. Part of that came from watching old Marx Brothers movies and reruns of Candid Camera. Eventually his disease subsided, his health returned, and Cousins is convinced it was his laughter and sustained focus on the bright side that brought about his healing.

We've found that the ability to be lighthearted helps us work through many heavy and difficult situations without burning out or losing our perspective. Humor is our release, our safety valve. Laughter relieves tension and breaks down barriers. Laughter is therapeutic. It is medicinal. It heals. It gives hope.

> A cheerful heart is good medicine, but a crushed spirit dries up the bones (Proverbs 17:22).

He who laughs, lasts.

CAN WORK BE FUN?

When you're done relaxing, of course, there's always work to come back to. But relaxation and work don't always have to be opposites. Work should be fulfilling and rewarding, not just a necessary evil. We saw a bumper sticker that says "The worst day fishing is better than the best day working." If this is true for you (substituting whatever you like for fishing), it's sad. Work is good—and if we can only learn when to leave it we will find greater fulfillment when we come back to it.

Slow down before you break down. Shake the hurry habit. Beware of the barrenness of busyness. Remind yourself that your Christian faith should be filling you with the joy of life, not robbing you of it.

A few years ago we ran across a reflection attributed in one source to an elderly woman, and in another to a monastery friar.[5] Whoever said it, we believe it offers a needed breath of lightness to Christian women weighed down under self-imposed stress, hesitant to take God's relaxation prescription:

> If I had my life to live over again, I'd try
>   to make more mistakes next time.
> I would relax, I would limber up, I would be sillier
>   than I have been this trip.
> I know of very few things I would take seriously.
> I would take more trips. I would be crazier.
> I would climb more mountains, swim more rivers,
>   and watch more sunsets.
> I would do more walking and looking.
> I would eat more ice cream and less beans.
> I would have more actual troubles, and fewer
>   imaginary ones.
> You see, I'm one of those people who lives life
>   sensibly hour after hour.
>   Day after day. Oh, I've had my moments, and if I
>   had to do it over again I'd have more of them.
> In fact, I'd try to have nothing else, just moments,
>   one after another, instead of living so many years
>   ahead each day. I've been one of those people
>   who never go anywhere without a thermometer, a
>   hot-water bottle, a gargle, a raincoat, aspirin,
>   and a parachute.
> If I had to do it over again I would go places, do
>   things, and travel lighter than I have.
> If I had my life to live over I would start barefooted
>   earlier in the spring and stay that way later in the fall.
> I would play hookey more.
> I wouldn't make such good grades, except by
>   accident.
> I would ride on more merry-go-rounds.
> I'd pick more daisies.

FOOD FOR THOUGHT AND DISCUSSION

1. What does the word *relaxation* do to you? What thoughts, feelings, or pictures does it bring to mind?

2. How does the way a small child looks at life (for example, the outdoors) differ from the way we as adults often look at it? Give an example if you can.

3. Do you agree with the idea that spending more time outdoors helps us to relax and enjoy life more? Why or why not?

4. What do you do personally that helps you to really relax?

5. What kind of music do you find relaxing? What kind makes you unsettled or tense?

6. Have you ever taken a mental vacation by visualization, as described in this chapter? If not, try it. How did it make you feel?

7. What questions would you ask and what advice might you give to the person who says "I just can't sleep at night"?

8. "Refusing to rest and relax on a regular basis is not only unhealthy, it's disobedient." Do you agree or disagree? What Scripture would you use to defend your answer?

9. How helpful is fun and laughter as an antidote to stress? (What do you think of the statement "He who laughs, lasts"?)

1. Claudia Wallis, "Stress," *Time*, 6 June 1983, p. 50.

2. A free catalog of these environmental sounds can be obtained from the Moss Music Group, Inc., 48 West 38th Street, New York, NY 10018. We especially enjoy "Solitudes," volumes one and two.

3. Claudia Wallis, pp. 53-54.

4. Norman Cousins, *Anatomy of an Illness* (New York: W. W. Norton & Co., 1983).

5. Tim Hansel, *When I Relax I Feel Guilty* (Elgin, Ill.: David C. Cook Publishing Co., 1981), pp. 44-45.

CONCLUSION:
PACE YOUR RACE

Some years ago the women's competition in the Hawaii Ironman triathlon had one of the most dramatic endings in sports history. Coming into the final stretch with a comfortable lead, the triathlete reached the very end of her reserves. She slowed, staggered, then collapsed within sight of the finish line. Her mind and body were barely functioning. It was a pathetic and frightening sight.

Determined to win she crawled toward the finish line, only to be passed by a competitor at the last moment.

The crowd and the commentators had the same reaction—too bad she lost. But even if she would have won, what a terrible price to pay.

This memorable moment illustrates a critical principle for Christian women today. Life is not a short distance to be run at a sprint with reckless abandon. It is a long distance to be run with care and thoughtfulness, saving bursts of speed for when they are necessary but giving yourself time to recover before the next burst. The twenty-six miles of a marathon must be run strategically, conserving energy, monitoring then pacing oneself according to energy reserves. Otherwise, no matter how fast we may have started the race, we will end up losers, collapsed in a heap short of the finish line.

Some of us are tortoises (type B's), some of us are hares (type A's). The hares run themselves ragged, pleased that they're getting more done and getting it done faster than the tortoises. The tortoises burn energy slowly but surely, getting the job done but not raising their blood pressure much in the process. While the hares start off with a great lead, they end up spending so much time sick, run down, and weighted down that the tortoises pass them by, getting more done in the long run, and in the process living longer lives and better lives.

Some cars are still going strong with 200,000 miles on them, others are sputtering at 60,000 miles and goners at 80,000. All of us need to go down some bumpy roads in life, and occasionally we need to speed. But if our throttles are always wide open, our feet perpetually to the floor, if our most traveled roads are all full of chuckholes . . . how long can we expect to last? How much mileage will we get out of our lives?

Christian stewardship is much more than what we do with our money. It begins with what we do with ourselves. We must see taking care of ourselves—spiritually, psychologically, and physically—as an investment. Barring accidents and diseases beyond our control, proper self-care lengthens our days.

God's words are called "life to those who find them and health to a man's whole body" (Proverbs 4:22). Apparently God is concerned about our health and longevity:

My son, do not forget my teaching,
but keep my commands in your heart,
for they will prolong your life many years
and bring you prosperity.
(Proverbs 3:1-2)

Listen, my son, accept what I say,
and the years of your life will be many.
(Proverbs 4:10)

The fear of the LORD is the beginning of wisdom,
and knowledge of the Holy One is understanding.
For through me your days will be many,
and years will be added to your life.
(Proverbs 9:10-11)

The fear of the LORD adds length to life,
but the years of the wicked are cut short.
(Proverbs 10:27)

If we live according to God's principles, we will withdraw in daily meditation, develop godly perspective, learn to manage our emotions, and learn to eat, exercise, and rest properly to care for our physical bodies, the temples of his spirit. Can living by God's prescription really help us live longer?

These are the commands, decrees and laws the LORD your God directed me to teach you to observe in the land that you are crossing the Jordan to possess, so that you, your children and their children after them may fear the LORD your God as long as you live by keeping all his decrees and commands that I give you, and *so that you may enjoy long life* (Deuteronomy 6:1-2, italics mine).

Of course, we have no guarantee of long life on this earth. God may have other plans, better plans for us. But let's put the emphasis on the word *enjoy* from the passage above. We're talking now not about quantity but quality of life. Those who pace themselves are invariably the most content and refreshed people. They have more to offer their families, their friends, their church, their ministry. They're more enjoyable to be

245

around, they enjoy being around, and—all things being equal—they're around longer to enjoy.

Women under stress must give their bodies and minds time and rest to recover. They need to cut back their responsibilities, be around positive and upbeat people, friends that they're comfortable with and don't have to perform for. They need extra help with the children, and extra help around the house until they recover. If you are such a woman, ask for help. If you know such a woman, offer help.

Suppose you had a serious accident that put you on your back for a month or two. You'd have to get some help and cut back on your activities, and you wouldn't expect to be walking normally for months to come. Likewise if you've been seriously stressed-out, you shouldn't expect to function at a normal level again for some time. Get out of bed too soon and you'll make that injured back worse and set back the healing process. Jump back into your normal pattern of living when you're worn ragged from stress, and you'll be sure to make it worse.

Sure, some women may pamper themselves unnecessarily and use stress as an excuse for avoiding their responsibilities. But we've talked with far more women who are so responsibility conscious, so totally devoted to their families and committed to their tasks, that they feel guilty caring for themselves. They think it's selfish to take a nap, and unspiritual to send out for pizza. They feel like at best it's an imposition and at worst a sin to ask for help. If it's you we're describing, you must change the way you think and start taking care of yourself . . . or you'll bequeath to that family you love a broken and burned-out woman.

When we're in a crisis, driving ourselves after our resources are depleted demonstrates bravery and perseverance. But when we're not in a crisis, it demonstrates foolishness. Please— get some help and give yourself some time and rest.

Jesus came that we might have abundant life, not just in heaven but on earth. How rich and rewarding is your life? How much more rich and rewarding could it be with a daily maintenance plan for the body, soul, and spirit God has entrusted to your care?

Let's open up the windows of our lives, learning not just to survive but thrive. Let's learn to pace our race, to pray and to live the words of Orin Crain:

Slow me down, Lord.

Ease the pounding of my heart by the quieting of my mind.

Steady my hurried pace with a vision of the eternal reach of time.

Give me, amid the confusion of the day, the calmness of the everlasting hills.

Break the tensions of my nerves and muscles with the soothing music of the singing streams that live in my memory.

Teach me the art of taking minute vacations—of slowing down to look at a flower, to chat with a friend, to pat a dog, to smile at a child, to read a few lines from a good book.

Slow me down, Lord, and inspire me to send my roots deep into the soil of life's enduring values, that I may grow toward my greater destiny.

Remind me each day that the race is not always to the swift; that there is more to life than increasing its speed.

Let me look upward to the towering oak and know that it grew great and strong because it grew slowly and well.

God made only one you, so budget yourself. Spend yourself wisely. Seek to be able to say to the Lord at the end of your life, "I have brought you glory on earth by completing the work you gave me to do" (John 17:4). No less. And no more.